*To Roy Hadfield*

*Your life was your legacy*

Published by MJF Books
Fine Communications
322 Eighth Avenue
New York, NY 10001

*Running for Mortals*
LC Control Number: 2011938931
ISBN-13: 978-1-60671-080-7
ISBN-10: 1-60671-080-X

The information in this book is meant to supplement, not replace, proper exercise training. All forms of exercise pose some inherent risks. The editors and publishers advise readers to take full responsibility for their safety and know their limits. Before practicing the exercises in this book, be sure that your equipment is well maintained, and do not take risks beyond your level of experience, aptitude, training, and fitness. The exercise and dietary programs in this book are not intended as a substitute for any exercise routine or dietary regimen that may have been prescribed by your doctor. As with all exercise and dietary programs, you should get your doctor's approval before beginning.

Printed in the United States of America.

MJF Books and the MJF colophon are trademarks of Fine Creative Media, Inc.

QF   10  9  8  7  6  5  4  3  2  1

# CONTENTS

## SECTION IV: BECOMING A BETTER RUNNER

## SECTION V: RUNNING FOR YOUR LIFE

## APPENDIX

# ACKNOWLEDGMENTS

When we sat down to write *Marathoning for Mortals*, it was a little like running an actual marathon for the first time. Although we had known each other for several years, we weren't really sure what to expect as we tried to combine our creative energies to write a book.

With the same kind of blissful naïveté that most first-timers experience, we wrote and laughed and busied ourselves through the entire manuscript. And when it was complete, we felt the relief and satisfaction that come from accomplishing the unknown.

This book was much like a second marathon. The good news is that you know what to expect. The bad news is that you know what to expect. No longer naïve, you experience every mile—every chapter—as an event of its own. And when it's finished, the feeling is more disbelief than relief.

There are people without whom this book could never have come to life. We'd like to thank Jim Luning, a wonderful photographer and motorcycle nut who took all the photos; and Teresa Nightingale, Web master supreme, who did the photo editing.

Thanks, too, to Brendan York, Adam Wille, and Jeff Haas, physical therapists at Athletico, for their help on the injury prevention chapter.

And a very special thanks to Kathy O'Malley for her unwavering support, her unconditional friendship, and the use of her country house to give us a quiet place to think and to write.

John and Jenny

# INTRODUCTION

Close your eyes and think of a runner. What do you see? If you see someone with 1 percent body fat sprinting alone down a deserted highway, then you need to keep reading. It ain't that way anymore.

Robert Fulghum writes that everything he really needs to know he learned in kindergarten. He learned, among other things, that it is important to play fair, to share, to put things back where you found them, and to flush the toilet.

We believe that we really learned everything we need to know about running well before we even *got* to kindergarten. As soon as we learned how to walk, we wanted to run. We knew as toddlers that the best way to get from where we were to where we wanted to be was to run there. It still is!

We knew as small children that running for no apparent reason at all was one of life's greatest pleasures. It still is.

The door would open, and we would run out. We ran around. We chased. We ran to and from. We ran until we couldn't run anymore, and then we stopped. That's still a pretty good plan.

Sometime in early childhood, though, many of us discovered that as much fun as running was for us, we really weren't all that good at it. We liked it. It felt good. We wanted to do it. But somehow, knowing that others were faster stole the joy from our running.

Eventually, many of us just stopped running. We stopped because we were afraid of the comparisons that others would make. We stopped because we were afraid we'd look silly or slow, or that others would make fun of us.

Those images of ourselves and of others are stuck in our minds. We see other people as runners but, for one reason or another, we do not see ourselves as runners. We see younger, fitter, faster people running, but not ourselves. Well, things have changed.

There's a revolution in running going on—a change that started slowly in the 1990s and has grown into a full-fledged revolution. It started on city paths and small-town streets. It started with a few brave men and women risking embarrassment by taking their enthusiasm for running out into the open and has led to the most dramatic increase in running participation in history.

The most recent *Runner's World* magazine survey suggests that there are nearly 24 million runners in the United States alone—*24 million runners*. You know that they can't all be the skinny, fast characters in your imagination. Today's runners are fast and slow, skinny and not so skinny, young, old, male, female, and every possible combination of the above.

Today's runners don't even always run. They run. They run-walk. They walk-run. Some simply walk. And that's the beauty of running today. You can be a runner even if running isn't what you do.

All it takes to be convinced is one look at the thousands of participants standing in the starting corrals of large long-distance running events. In the giant entertainment events, like the Rock 'n' Roll Marathon, nearly 20,000 men and woman—your friends, neighbors, and colleagues—will accept the challenge with bodies no better suited to the distance than yours.

They've accepted the challenge because they can. They already know what you're about to discover: that anyone with a willing spirit can be a runner today. Anyone, of any age, of any weight, can begin the process of becoming a runner. It's as simple as wanting to run, planning to run, and then running.

Why you run isn't nearly as important as the fact that you run. If you're like many of the people we encounter in our training programs and online, you're thinking about running to help you lose weight. The years and choices are beginning to take their toll. If that's why you want to run, you've come to the right place.

Some of you may want to shape up. Maybe your body has begun to look more like how you remember your older relatives looked. You remember, don't you? Remember that one old aunt whose sagging arm kept waving long after she had stopped saying good-bye?

A few of you may even be looking for a new challenge. Maybe you've hit that point in your life where you're wondering what comes next.

Whatever your reason to run, you have already taken the most difficult step you're ever going to take. You've made the decision—tentatively, perhaps—to find out what it will take to become a runner. No step from here forward will ever be as difficult.

The plain truth is that the only thing you have to do to be a runner is run. As obvious as that sounds, you'd be shocked at how few people fully grasp the elegant simplicity of the sport.

You don't need long legs or narrow hips. You don't need powerful muscles or ripped abs. You don't need a superhuman heart or lungs. You don't need anything other than willingness.

What's the catch? Aha . . . You're right. There is a catch. The catch is—and there's no way to escape this—you have to learn to run in the body that you're in right now. Those legs that you use every day are the legs of a runner. They're neither too short nor too long; they just are.

The same is true of the rest of your body. It's also true of your mind and your spirit. You are the one who will have to become a runner: you—just you. There's no secret weapon, no magic pill, no flash of insight that will allow you to transcend what you are.

All of you will have to become a runner, not just the parts of you that actually run. It doesn't do any good to have the legs of a runner if you have the soul of a nonrunner. It won't do you a bit of good to train your body to accept new challenges and rewards if you leave your mind as it is. It is a total commitment. It is a full engagement of body, mind, emotion, and spirit.

Today's runner is more than just an athlete. Today's runner is athlete, coach, philosopher, poet, and storyteller. Today's runner understands that the old days of doing what someone else expected of you are long gone. Today's runner knows that the search for one's own excellence and potential must be undertaken alone.

We are your guides. We can't show you your path, but we can tell you about ours. We can show you where we made our mistakes and where you might be inclined to make yours. We can tell you about our joys and frustrations, our stunning successes, and our agonizing failures. We can tell you because we've been there.

Throughout the book, we will make suggestions. We will lay out the plans and programs we think will help you achieve your goals. We will give you the information we think you need to make better decisions about what you eat and how you move.

We will give you the tips, tools, and techniques we've acquired from thousands of people just like you. Some of these suggestions will make sense to you; some of them will seem really dumb. It doesn't matter. What makes sense, you can try. What seems dumb, you can hold off on.

What matters is that you start to find out what works for you and what doesn't. It's important that you learn what makes you feel better and what makes you feel worse. It's important that you help yourself become the runner you want to be.

We'll be here to point the way, warn you of the dangers, and help you avoid the most obvious mistakes. We'll be honest with you so that you can learn how to be honest with yourself.

Once you turn the page, there will be no going back. Your past will be behind you. And day by day, one step at a time, you are going to move forward toward who you want to be. You'll be changing your life with your own two feet.

You will be becoming a runner.

Giddyap.

# SECTION I

## GETTING STARTED

# 1

# MEET YOUR GUIDES

## PENGUIN PEARLS OF WISDOM

*The miracle isn't that I finished. The miracle is that I had the courage to start.*

Those two sentences changed my life—and the lives of thousands who have read them. They sum up for so many of us what is really in our hearts.

To prepare and finish is not a miracle. With patience and good humor, all of us can achieve our dreams.

The miracle is that we were able to reach down and find some part of ourselves that still believed our dreams were possible.

## MEET JOHN "THE PENGUIN" BINGHAM

I am probably the least likely person you can imagine to write a book about running. For most of my life, I thought runners were some crazy subset of humans. *Why,* I wondered, *would anyone willingly subject himself or herself to the pain of running?*

You see, my own running career—and I like to call it a running career—didn't begin until I was 43 years old. At 43, I was overweight (some 75 pounds more than I am right now), and I had smoked for 25 years and done more than my fair share of drinking.

I also grew up in a family in which overeating was a way of life. In my family, food was everywhere. Food was love. Food was celebration. Food was everything except food.

Whatever happened in our family, we ate. Sue and Mart got married? Let's eat. Betsy had a baby? Let's eat. In fact, there was nothing that was so horrible that you couldn't eat your way through it. Wakes and funerals were just occasions to set up the smorgasbord table.

I am asked all the time: What happened? How does a sedentary, middle-aged smoker/drinker/overeater suddenly decide to start moving, quit smoking, stop drinking, and change his eating habits? Well, the sad truth is that I don't have a great answer.

There wasn't some magical moment of epiphany and enlightenment when I realized that my life had gotten out of control. I had never been athletic, so it wasn't as if the "ghost of fitness past" visited me in the middle of the night and reminded me of how good I used to be.

And the additional truth is that when you have as many bad habits as I had, you can't always change all of them at the same time. Getting more active and changing my eating style was the easy part. The smoking and the drinking were habits that I had to sneak up on before I could make the changes stick.

It's not as if I had been living on the planet Xenon. I knew that my eating, drinking, and smoking—not to mention the complete absence of any kind of exercise—did not make the healthiest lifestyle. I knew all of that; I just didn't want to do anything about it.

Well, that's not completely true. I did—like so many others—get fired up from time to time and decide to lose weight. Some diet program would grab my attention, and I would be committed to following it to the letter.

I tried high-protein, low-carbohydrate diets and low-protein, high-carbohydrate diets ("the athlete's diet," I was told). I mixed up drinks I could barely swallow and put foul-smelling powder on the worse-tasting yogurt, all in the name of slimming down.

Nothing worked for very long. But I did manage to create three wardrobes. I had my "fat" clothes, my "thin" clothes, and my uniforms from army infantry basic training that I knew I would never get back into.

I even tried running once or twice. And that was about it—once or twice. I hated it and I quit.

This time, though, I was determined to become a runner. As I stood in my driveway, the depth of my ignorance began to set in. I had no idea what to do. And why would I? They never show old fat men running on television—never. The only running I had ever seen on TV was at the Olympics, and those people were all young and skinny.

But I was there, and I had to do something. I figured runners must just run as fast as they can as far as they can every time they run. I stood there for a while, and then, with a primal scream, I headed down my driveway at full speed.

For about 8 seconds, my driveway, which was only about 50 yards long, suddenly looked like it stretched to the horizon. It took 8 seconds for me to end up bent over, gasping for air, hacking and coughing and wondering what in the world I had gotten myself into.

Looking back, I know that was my moment of truth. That was my moment of choice. Behind me was the life I knew. I owned nine motorcycles, two cars, a camper, a garden tractor, and a gas-powered Weedwacker. I had been in no danger of exerting myself.

Everything I knew about myself was behind me. The cigarettes, the booze, the indulgent lifestyle . . . All I had to do was turn around and end the folly.

Much to my surprise, I straightened up and went forward into the abyss. I ran a little, walked a lot, and stumbled as far as I thought I could go. When I turned around to make sure I knew where I was, I could still see my house. I had given it my all—my very best effort—and I couldn't even get out of sight of my house!

But it was a beginning. It was *my* beginning. Strangely enough, it turns out that I had promise as a runner on that very first day. It was clear that I didn't have a runner's body, but I possessed a runner's mind. You see, when I returned home, I got into my car and measured how far I had run.

One quarter of a mile.

Every day or so I'd put on my way-too-small shoes and head out the door. Little by little, I made progress. I stopped wearing the jacket, wool cap, and ski gloves and ran just a little farther every time I went out.

I ran in the morning or evening, when I felt most certain that I wouldn't be seen. In fact, if a car approached, I always pretended to be looking for something along the side of the road. I was convinced that the sight of this old fat man running in a sweat suit would be enough to send the driver into fits of laughter.

In those early days and weeks, I was fueled more by anger and frustration than anything else. I couldn't believe what I had done to myself. And I had done it to myself by myself.

But everything good that running has brought into my life started from those humble beginnings. Running the original marathon course in Athens; running in the heart of Florence, Italy, or on the stony ground of Antarctica—it all started with those first 8 seconds.

Without those first 8 seconds, there would be no New York City or Chicago Marathon. There would be no column in *Runner's World*, and there would be no books to write. Without those first 8 seconds, I would have sentenced myself to a life of sedentary confinement. I would have continued to eat, drink, and smoke until I couldn't move at all.

All we're asking for is those first 8 seconds of *your* life. And you can take my word for it that no matter what those first 8 seconds feel like, they are going to change your life forever.

## MEET COACH JENNY HADFIELD

I used to love to run. I ran after my friends while playing tag, kicked the can on the neighborhood streets, and played a mean game of "duck, duck, goose" in kindergarten. It wasn't until I grew into my body later in life that I developed a love/hate relationship with running. I loved the romance of running and wanted to be a runner, but I hated it every time I tried.

I was an active but chubby adolescent. I loved team sports like volleyball, softball, and basketball. Yet every time I tried to run, I failed. For me, running was a form of punishment I had to endure in sports. If we missed serves, we *had* to run laps. If we missed a layup, we *had* to run laps. We *had* to run laps to warm up for a softball game. It was something I *had* to do for a short period of time. I hated that it was so hard, but I wanted desperately to learn how to run.

My initial attempts at becoming a runner were short-lived. I would strap on my shoes, head out to run, and end up walking back before I even got to the end of the block. John would agree that I can be quite the stubborn one, but every time I tried to run, the end result was the same. I couldn't imagine myself as a runner.

It wasn't until after college that I finally conquered my mental block against running. I was an intern at a corporate fitness center—GE Medical Systems—teaching employees how to get and stay fit. The entire fitness center staff ran. They ran at lunch together, they ran on the weekends with a club, and they even ran races! I wanted in. I wanted to feel what they felt when they finished their runs. They glowed; they were high on life; they were real runners.

I shared my aspirations, and they took me under their wings and taught me how to get started. It wasn't 10 minutes into the first run-walk that they were asking me to run Al's Run, a local 8-K (5-mile) road race in Milwaukee. The idea scared the pants off me. I told them, "I can't run that far, and even if I did, I would be the last person out there." I told them, "At this point, I'll be lucky to make it to the end of this street."

It was during that run that they guided me gently into my running career. They talked to me about progression, how to train, how to rest. They took me shopping for running shoes and clothing so I looked the part. Week by week, my body adapted and my mind broke down the barriers. It took me several months to run 30 minutes straight, and although I was feeling a little more confident, the thought of running in a race was daunting.

On a crisp fall morning in Milwaukee, I lined up for my first race. I didn't know what to expect. I didn't believe I would finish. I worried that if I finished at all, I would finish last. I was completely out of my comfort zone but excited with anticipation. It took me well over an hour to finish the race, and I was beaten at the finish line by a 72-year-old man named Harry, but I finished. I felt like I'd won the lottery—like I'd opened a door I never knew was there. I learned to run, I ran a race, and I had a T-shirt to prove it!

I share that story with you because all too often I hear from people who think they can't run but want to try. I am living proof that you can. You can run for fun, to meet new people, or even to run a race. Running gave me the confidence to explore life and step out of my comfort zone. I went on to run more races and further challenge myself in other sports. Running is not just exercise; it is a lifestyle.

Join us on the journey into our world of running. Set your worries aside, and learn from our successes and failures. We will guide you through everything you need to know to get started, to improve, and to become your own coach. Taking the first step is the most challenging part. It is that step that will lead you into a whole new world.

## COACH JENNY'S TIPS AND TRICKS

✓ Remember that it generally takes 20 days to create a new habit. Gather up your patience, read up on running, and give yourself a good month to start your running career.

✓ Begin to think like a runner. What will you look like running? Where are you going to run? Who will you run with? More important, what will you wear?

✓ Talk to runners you admire. Listen to their stories of how they got started. In most cases, their tales won't be far off from your story. Being a runner isn't based on distance or speed. You share the same strengths and weaknesses as the elite runners. A real runner is one who puts aside his or her fears and heads out the door.

# 2

# THE WONDERFUL WORLD OF RUNNING

We live in a runner's world. We live in a world of runners. It sounds like the same thing, but it's not. Let us try to explain.

The world of running has changed so much in the past 20 years that old-school, hidebound runners don't even recognize it anymore. For them, it's a little like going back to the old neighborhood and finding out that the houses you knew have all been torn down, and new condominiums have taken their place.

Running used to be an elitist sport. It was populated only by those with the physical gifts and mental energy to become runners and continue running. In the old days, running was no place for the timid, the thin-skinned, the noncompetitive, or the social person. It was hard-core all the way.

In those days, the goal of nearly every running workout was to push yourself to your absolute limit—every time. You showed up, ran hard, and exhausted yourself; you ran through pain and injury, and you suffered because that's what runners did.

These were what we call the "nylon shorts runners." You still find some of them out on the running paths and in races today, although you don't see nearly as many as you might expect. These were the club runners, the age-groupers; they were mostly men who defined themselves through their running.

Training runs were mini races. What started as gentle, easy-paced runs quickly turned into testosterone-fueled battles of bodies, spirits, and wills. Life for a runner in those days was pretty easy: You were either winning or losing. There was no in between.

Many new runners still imagine that runner's world. We did. And it's an intimidating place. It's terrifying to think that the only way you can call yourself a runner is if you're willing to sacrifice it all every day. Most of us just can't do that. And nearly all of us shouldn't.

We're a part of the *new* running generation. We used to be called the Second Running Boom. The old-school runners called us a boom because they were sure that we'd go bust. They never imagined that we'd keep running for a lifetime.

This new generation is just a little bit older, with maybe just a little more perspective on what running is—and isn't—in our lives. Running isn't the be-all and end-all of our existence. Our lives and happiness don't revolve around the last run or next personal record (PR, as it's called—one's best time over a given distance).

In fact, what surprises many of the first-generation runners is how happy we in the second generation are. We Gen 2 runners seem quite content to run and walk and waddle our way through our training runs and races. We somehow find a way to smile through 90-minute 10-Ks and 6-hour marathons.

New runners come in all shapes and sizes, from different backgrounds, and with varied athletic experience. New runners are young single men and women with good jobs and fast-track careers. New runners are women and men with families. New runners are thin and not so thin; they are too tall and too short and too old and in too bad a shape to run. But they do.

They run for the same reasons you want to run. They run because they think they can. They run because they're afraid they can't, because someone told them they should, or because someone told them they shouldn't.

Gen 2 runners already know what you're about to find out: that life is just better as a runner.

Today's running world is a warm, supportive, cooperative place where friends gather to celebrate each other's accomplishments. It's a world where we as runners focus on the aspects of our lives that bind us together, rather than the meaningless data like speed and distance that separate us from each other.

And how could it be any other way? How can anyone define success and achievement and accomplishment for anyone but themselves? And why would they try, except to put themselves in a place of superiority? It may be that this generation of runners is fundamentally different from the previous generation.

In today's running community, *you* define success. You define what it means to be a runner—first and foremost. And that's the beauty of the running community. All you need to do to join is run.

If it's early in your running career—and we were all beginners once—just getting out the door three times a week may be a life-altering achievement. Today's running community will celebrate that with you.

Through this book, we are going to help you learn to celebrate yourself. We are going to help you learn to think and act and feel like a member of the running community.

We also live in a world of runners, and what a world it is. The people who are around us—who work with us and play with us; who have shared our joys and disappointments, our successes and our failures—are all runners.

The runners in our world are as different as they could be. They are young and old, fast and slow, male and female, and it doesn't matter. They are who they are and nothing more. They are who they are and nothing less.

One of the runners in our world is a young Kenyan named Daniel. Daniel is an elite athlete. He runs well. He runs fast. He runs—like a Kenyan. Daniel grew up in Africa running barefoot, without coaches or organized races or any of the other elements that we might consider necessary. He ran because he could. He ran because his running made him who he wanted to be. He ran because through his running, he could find a better place.

But Daniel, as gifted and talented and dedicated as he is, is no different than you are—or we were—as you read this book. Daniel at some point had to decide to become a runner. He had to take the same risk that you are taking. He had to choose between being a runner and not being a runner. He, like you, had to choose between a lifestyle that included running and one that didn't.

Another of the runners in our world we call Johnnie Hands. Johnnie's running career started more like most of ours—with all the cards stacked up against him. We nicknamed him Johnnie Hands because he ran wearing giant ski gloves. Johnnie was about as far from being a runner as you can imagine. He was overweight and out of shape, with enough bad habits for three or four people. But he was also determined.

The first time he ran with our learn-to-run group, he couldn't—or wouldn't—stop talking. His feet were shuffling on the ground, but his mouth was going a mile a minute. He wanted to know everything, and he wanted to know it right now. He wanted to know how to run, how far to run, how fast to run. He wanted to know what shoes, what shorts, what kind of shirt he should have. He wanted to know how to look like a runner even before he *was* a runner.

Johnnie, like most of us, wanted it all and he wanted it now. He was having so much fun that he never wanted to stop. He couldn't believe what was happening to him. He couldn't believe how good it felt to run 3 miles, then 4, then 10 and beyond.

In no time at all, Johnnie found himself running with the same passion and abandon that he had lived the rest of his life. The problem was, for Johnnie and the rest of us, that the body doesn't always keep up with the mind.

Johnnie struggled. It's not easy for any of us to overcome our histories, and he was no exception. His enthusiasm was his greatest asset and his greatest liability. He was, in some ways, his biggest hurdle to becoming a runner. So Johnnie had some setbacks. He had a few minor aches and pains that turned into nagging injuries that turned into a learning experience on how to—and how not to—run.

A girlfriend finds that running is a way to get from where she was to where she wants to be. She runs to find herself; she runs because only running allows her to be who she really is.

A middle-aged male friend runs because he wants to keep his weight down. He likes to have a beer now and then and figures that running is one way to balance his indulgences.

Another friend, who has lost more than 150 pounds, runs because she lives in fear that she'll wake up one morning and all the weight will have come back. She runs to keep the demons at bay.

The list goes on and on. Soon you'll be able to add your name to this list of runners in our world.

Our world—the running world—is filled with people just like you, no matter who you are or where you're beginning your journey. We have coached and mentored and guided thousands of ordinary people—people with jobs and families and loads of bad habits—and seen them all transformed into runners.

The simple truth is that you can be a runner if you want to be one. No one can stop you. No one can tell you that you're not good enough. No one can tell you that you're not fast enough or that you don't run far enough. No one (but yourself) can keep you out of this wonderful world we live in. For us, running and runners are our entire world. We live our lives as runners and with runners. But it doesn't have to be that way for you.

The world of running and the runners in that world are waiting to welcome you with open arms. They have been through everything that you'll go through. They will see the fear and joy in your eyes, and it will remind them of their own early running experiences.

But the most amazing part of becoming a runner and becoming part of this running world is that someday you too will look back on this beginning and remember. Someday you too will reach back to help someone else who is struggling with what you're struggling with today.

In time, you will be the one to whom newer runners turn for advice. You will be the model, the example, the hero to those who haven't yet made the discoveries you're about to make.

You are about to step across the threshold into the most terrifying and satisfying adventure of your life. You are going to run into yourself.

## COACH JENNY'S TIPS AND TRICKS

✓ If you are new to running, head to a local race finish line and cheer for the runners or be a volunteer to set up water stations or work in the medical tent for the race. Being there will ease your nerves about whether you fit in and motivate you to get started.

✓ Contact your local running store or club and join a fun run. This is a great way to meet runners and get in a great workout too!

✓ Avoid comparing yourself to someone else. You are on your own journey, and only you can define the path you're going to take. It's never too late to learn to run or return to running. I've coached new runners in their seventies. Excuses aside, running is a very friendly activity and, besides walking, the most primal exercise there is.

✓ The key is to recognize your own level and start running accordingly, be patient while you progress, and stick with it. It will pay off in the long run. If it were easy, everyone would be running.

✓ Develop your own running schedule. Mix it with yoga classes or cycling sessions. Incorporate running into your lifestyle and before you know it, it will feel as routine as brushing your teeth.

# 3

# DISCOVERING YOURSELF: THE GOOD, BAD, AND UGLY

## PENGUIN PEARLS OF WISDOM

*Through running, we rediscover what we knew as children: that being safe all the time doesn't make for a very interesting hour or day. And it makes for a very uninteresting life. The fun is at the edge of the unknown.*

We all knew as children that taking risks was an important part of growing up. We wanted to cross the street to find out what was on the other side.

As adults, too often our natural curiosity is overcome by fear. We know who we are now, but we are afraid of what we might discover we can be.

This is less about running and more about you. Take this opportunity to define yourself in your own terms. Let your feet carry you back to yourself—and then ahead to who you *can* be.

My first attempt at running as a young woman didn't last very long. I didn't think about how far I should go; I didn't think about how hard I should run; I just ran. I made it to just about the end of our street and had to turn back humbly. I didn't have a plan. I couldn't figure out why I was unsuccessful. It was because I didn't start by first realistically evaluating my goals and expectations.

As a coach, I often see people put the cart before the horse. They sign up for a learn-to-run program and want to start by running right away. Some of us are able to begin with a little running, while others may need to start with walking or by mixing running with walking. Once I figured out where to start my running program, I successfully progressed to finishing a 5-mile race!

In order to get to where you are going, you've got to start with where you are now. For example, some of us were a little more gifted in the smarts category in school and skipped ahead, but most of us progressed one grade at a time, until we finally graduated from high school.

Unless you're a genius, you can't learn geometry in first grade. You need to go through all the lessons in mathematics first and then progress to the harder stuff. Likewise, our bodies need to graduate from no activity to some activity to regular activity. For runners, this is especially true because running is a high-impact sport. Doing too much too soon can only hurt you. Believe me, I've experimented and only know by my mistakes.

Becoming a runner happens over time, like going through grade school. Each week, the body adapts and learns how to run a little farther or a little faster. A smart running program builds little by little, making sure not to tip the scales while adding just enough stress to progress and grow stronger. In physiology, this is known as the 10 percent rule. Based on research, it states that it is optimal to increase mileage by no more than 10 percent each week. Staying within those guidelines ensures a safe and effective progression week by week and decreases the risk of overuse injuries. When you put the whole puzzle together, it looks like a series of rolling hills, increasing and decreasing, building, and resting.

For most of us, this is the hardest part of running—the part where we have to do a little and wait a lot. In today's fast-paced world, we are used to getting things so quickly that becoming a runner seems like a very slow process. However, if you focus on the journey rather than how far or how fast you are going, time will fly, and you will be able to see tangible results as you go.

You may start with a little running and walking, add rest, and hold it at that level for a few weeks. Like a garden, your body will adapt and grow stronger. Then we'll add a little more running. A little goes a long way in becoming a runner. It should never be painful, make you miserable, or cause you to swear out loud!

Sometimes our motivation to push becomes greater than our bodies can handle. When this happens, injuries occur. Life then becomes less about running and more about rehabbing. Although injuries are at times an unavoidable element of running, your attention to your body's needs and abilities can help you avoid days lost to nursing unnecessary injuries.

Running is more about listening to your body and less about following a program to the exact mile or minute. Successful runners and walkers figure that out from the beginning. They listen closely and continually modify their programs to allow their bodies to recover.

It's a lot like creating your own recipe. You may add more running minutes to one workout and more strength and flexibility training to another. You may find that, like John, you enjoy run-walking rather than running continuously. The ultimate goal is to figure out what works for you and stick with it.

Identifying the right plan for you involves taking a personal inventory of what you have and what you will need to pack on this journey. It requires getting to know yourself and assessing your assets and liabilities, such as how old you are, how often you move, and how many dings or dents you've acquired through the years. The first step is to complete what we call the Personal Inventory Form. What are your wants, needs, and goals? What is your exercise and injury history?

Everyone is different, and each of us should follow a program that makes the most sense based on this inventory of information. There is no one magic running program to satisfy everyone's needs. Sure, you can follow a program out there in the virtual world, but will it push you to an injury or not even prepare you at all? How do you know it will match your health history, exercise history, and goals?

The smartest way to begin is to take a long, hard look inside. Where are you now? Where do you want to go? What do you have to work with? What needs a little work? It is all about personalizing a program to meet your needs and expectations—a lot like shopping for a home. You don't want a home that is too small or too large. You don't want a home that will break your pocketbook. You shop for a home that suits your lifestyle, budget, and personality. You look for a home that fits you and your stuff.

The following questions are geared to help you gather personal information about your past, present, and future. The key here is to answer honestly and thoroughly. The more honest you are, the more tailored your running program will be. Your answers will guide you in making a smart decision about which program suits your needs.

This Personal Inventory Form can be used as you progress through various programs. It can help you evaluate where you've improved and where you still need improvement.

**What is your age?**
- ☐ 18 to 30
- ☐ 31 to 40
- ☐ 41 to 50
- ☐ 51 or older

## What is your gender?

☐ Female

☐ Male

## What is your weight?

☐ My weight is appropriate for my height; I don't consider myself overweight.

☐ I am less than 10 pounds over my ideal weight.

☐ I am 10 to 25 pounds over my ideal weight.

☐ I am 25 to 50 pounds over my ideal weight.

☐ I am more than 50 pounds over my ideal weight.

## Describe your general health.

☐ I have never had any health problems.

☐ I have been under a doctor's care for ailments but am currently healthy.

☐ I am under a doctor's care for a chronic medical condition.

☐ I will be lucky to get to the end of the day.

## Describe your injury history.

☐ I have never had an injury in my life.

☐ I have had injuries, but they healed fine.

☐ I am currently under a doctor's care (or should be) for an injury.

☐ I am in complete denial about my injuries, even though I can barely walk.

## Describe your activity level.

☐ I participate in some form of continuous (without breaks) aerobic activity most days (4 to 6) of the week.

□ I participate in some form of continuous aerobic activity some days (1 to 3) of the week.

□ I have participated in continuous aerobic activity but never been consistent.

□ Opening this book is the most exercise I've had in 6 months.

**Describe your past activity level.**

□ I have been active for more than 1 year.

□ I have been active for more than 6 months.

□ I have been active for a few months.

□ I have been active for a few minutes.

**Decribe your past experience with running.**

□ I have never run before in my life.

□ I have run a little here and there but never consistently.

□ I have run on and off for years.

□ I run regularly three to five times per week.

□ I run like Forrest Gump, across countries for miles and miles at a time.

**How many days per week can you commit to training?**

□ 5

□ 3 or 4

□ 2 or 3

□ None or 1

**How many hours per week can you commit to training?**

□ 8 to 10

□ 6 to 8

☐ 4 to 6

☐ Fewer than 4

What are the top two or three factors that motivate you to exercise? (Examples: "weight loss," "training with a group," "following a structured program," "stress relief," "time for myself," or "having a goal to reach for.")

_____

_____

_____

List your short- and long-term goals for running.

_____

_____

_____

What will be your top challenges in following the training program? (Examples: "lack of time," "lack of motivation," or "lack of support.")

_____

_____

_____

We recommend writing the questions and answers on a separate piece of paper and keeping it in this book. You will be asked from time to time to go back to your answers to make sure that the course you've chosen is the course you want to be on.

If you've answered the questions honestly, you already have a head start on most participants in running programs because you'll be where you need to be. Lining up at the front in a 5-K won't help many first-time runners. Lining up in the middle to back of the pack will teach you how to pace and successfully run the race.

When you're ready, turn the page, and let's start making the plan.

## COACH JENNY'S TIPS AND TRICKS

✓ Keep your list of goals in plain sight—somewhere you can see them daily.

✓ Be honest and realistic with regard to your goals, abilities, and dreams. You will get to where you want to be a lot faster and have a lot more fun too!

✓ Talk through your running plan with your doctor. He or she may have some suggestions for how to exercise more safely.

✓ Let your friends and family know what your goals are and how they can help support you, whether by riding next to you on a bike or understanding you need the time alone to run.

✓ Find a friend to run with you if you are motivated by the social aspects of activity. You'll have more fun keeping each other on track.

# 4

# PICKING YOUR PATH

*I know it is important to start in the right place, but how do I know which training program is best for me?* Great question. As a running coach, I develop programs for a variety of runners and walkers. I create some programs for seasoned or experienced runners and others for new runners. It's nearly impossible to train all shapes and sizes with a single program. But you can plug yourself into a variety of plans, with differences in intensity or distance or goals, such as weight loss.

I review the Personal Inventory Form of each participant and suggest the safest running program for him or her. We'll do this together, and by the end of the chapter, you will know where to start and how to progress. The more patient and wise you are from the start, the faster your progression will be.

The following is a fictional new runner's personal inventory and details explaining why we are asking these questions.

• • • • • • • • • • • • • • • • • • • • • • • • • • • • • • • • • • • • • • • • • • • • • • • • • • • • • • • • • • • • • • • • • • • •

**Meet Ima Runner, a 39-year-old mother of two who wants to learn how to run. Ima has been inactive for months and wants to lose weight.**

**What is your age?**

- ☐ 18 to 30
- ☐ 31 to 40
- ☐ 41 to 50
- ☐ 51 or older

**Ima Runner's answer:** I am 39 years old.

• • • • • • • • • • • • • • • • • • • • • • • • • • • • • • • • • • • • • • • • • • • • • • • • • • • • • • • • • • • • • • • • • • • •

Ima's age is relevant to selecting a running program because as we age, our bodies can still perform but need more time to heal. Aches and pains last longer, so the nature of the program is to include a little more rest between runs.

Imagine a pyramid of life. The incline of the pyramid represents years 1 to 30; the decline illustrates 30 and over. On one side we are improving continually, while on the other, we are declining slowly. This is not a lesson designed to lead you into a deep depression but, rather, to explain what we have to work with relative to age.

Runners in their twenties can get away with a lot more mileage and less rest. The body is more resilient and bounces back quickly. Once we hit our thirties, our bodies need a little more time to recover from workout to workout. With youth we have energy and vitality, but with age comes the wisdom to train smart and listen to the body.

....................................................................

**What is your gender?**

☐ Female
☐ Male

**Ima Runner's answer:** Female.

....................................................................

We are all the same to some extent, but when it comes to gender there are, well, a few differences. I learned this during my years of adventure racing—a sport that includes coed teams of four; lots of miles (sometimes 300-plus); and paddling, biking, navigating, running, trekking, ropes, and any other challenges the race designers can think of. Racing taught me the subtle and not-so-subtle differences between men and women in sports. Men have the strength I wish I could have. Testosterone seems to run through their bodies like gasoline in a car, fueling their strong bodies and minds. Men get in shape faster than women, can run and walk faster, and hold all the records.

Women have a little testosterone, but for the most part it's estrogen running rampant through our bodies. Women can't leap over tall buildings in a single bound, but they *can* go on forever aerobically and have an incredibly high pain threshold. Women have the fat stores to support survival for days, weeks, and sometimes months. (I never thought I would be thankful for the extra fat here and there until I starting racing for days at a time. Then I realized why women are built the way we are: to survive, to nuture, and to protect.)

All you have to do to see the differences between the strengths of men and women is compare the finishing times for a 5-K, then a marathon, and then a 100-mile ultra marathon: Men hold 5-K and marathon records, while Ann Trason has won the overall category in ultra marathoning. So we all have our strengths; we just need to learn how to tap into them to benefit performance.

Guys, remember that from the very beginning, you can run fast. But it's not always wise to come in first. Your body needs to acquire the mileage base to support this urge. Ladies, remember that you can run for miles and burn lots of calories, but doing so without gradually increasing your distance will not necessarily drop the pounds the way you might think. In fact, it just may push you to burnout or injury. Whether you're male or female, be smart, be patient, and learn to use your strength and endurance to benefit your program.

......................................................................

**What is your weight?**

☐ My weight is appropriate for my height; I don't consider myself overweight.

☐ I am less than 10 pounds over my ideal weight.

☐ I am 10 to 25 pounds over my ideal weight.

☐ I am 25 to 50 pounds over my ideal weight.

☐ I am more than 50 pounds over my ideal weight.

**Ima Runner's answer:** I am 10 to 25 pounds over my ideal weight.

......................................................................

This may well be the most difficult question to answer honestly, not because you intend to be dishonest, but because we are sometimes out of touch with our weight and where it should be.

The important thing to understand here is that Ima is carrying extra weight as she starts her running program. Extra weight can be reduced with the right intensity and frequency, allowing her to run or walk more efficiently eventually. Because her main goal is to lose weight, Ima will start with Phase I of the Running for Mortals Weight Loss Program, a 12-week plan that includes walking and builds gradually to run-walking. This approach will teach her body how to adapt to the impact of running, reduce her risk of injury, and ultimately allow her to progress readily. Her patience will have to take precedent over her motivation to run. She will eventually progress through Phases II and III of the Weight Loss Program.

**Describe your general health condition.**
- ☐ I have never had any health problems.
- ☐ I have been under a doctor's care for ailments but am currently healthy.
- ☐ I am under a doctor's care for a chronic medical condition.
- ☐ I will be lucky to get to the end of the day.

**Ima Runner's answer:** I have been under a doctor's care for ailments but am currently healthy.

Ima had twins 3 years ago and was under a doctor's care for the duration of her pregnancy. Although she is now healthy, she still struggles with losing the weight she gained and occasionally suffers from back pain. Therefore, her pregnancies, even though they're in the past, are still a factor today.

Phase I of the Weight Loss Program also includes 2 days of strength and flexibility workouts. This part of Ima's program will strengthen her core muscles (abs and back), reduce back pain, and build lean muscle tissue to boost metabolism so she can lose weight.

Your past or present health is an important factor when considering training programs. Ailments such as diabetes, knee pain, low back pain, or a heart condition should be considered before the training process begins. It is highly recommended that you advise your doctor about your intention to begin an exercise program. Take the time to review your current health and discuss your past with your doctor, who can give you specific tips on modifications to your training program.

....................................................................

**Describe your injury history.**
- ☐ I have never had an injury in my life.
- ☐ I have had injuries, but they healed well.
- ☐ I am currently under a doctor's care (or should be) for an injury.
- ☐ I am in complete denial about my injuries even though I can barely walk.

**Ima Runner's answer:** I have had injuries, but they healed well.

....................................................................

After having her babies, Ima decided to try running to lose weight. Three weeks into her program, she developed pain in the bottom of her right knee. She was diagnosed with runner's knee and told to rest and ice it. She got discouraged while resting the injury and hasn't run since.

There are a couple of things at play here. One, running too soon drastically increases the likelihood of an injury early in the game. Ima's body was not used to the impact, and she was also carrying more weight than she had in the past. Her body simply raised a red flag to warn her that she was headed down the wrong path.

Listing past or present aches or pains or diagnosed injuries will help you determine what to watch out for as you progress. Aches and pains will be addressed along the way. Your body uses this amazing communication channel to tell your mind that you are pushing too hard too fast. Ignoring the red flags can only make things worse. In most cases, running through pain will make injuries worse or even cause other areas to hurt because you are overcompensating. Pain doesn't always mean you have to stop; it might just mean you need to be more in touch with your body and pay attention when it sends signals. In most cases, taking a few days off and allowing your injury to heal will take care of the problem.

**Describe your activity level.**

- ☐ I participate in some form of continuous (without breaks) aerobic activity most days (4 to 6) of the week.
- ☐ I participate in some form of continuous aerobic activity some days (1 to 3) of the week.
- ☐ I have participated in continuous aerobic activity but have never been consistent.
- ☐ Opening this book is the most exercise I've had in 6 months.

**Ima Runner's answer:** I participated in some activity more than a year ago.

**Describe your past activity level.**

- ☐ I have been active for more than 1 year.
- ☐ I have been active for more than 6 months.
- ☐ I have been active for a few months.
- ☐ I have been active for a few minutes.

**Ima Runner's answer:** I am currently inactive.

Ima tried almost everything, but her greatest challenge was sticking to an exercise program consistently. She walked; she ran; she participated in step, boxing, and even judo classes. She wants more than anything to be able to stick with a program and succeed.

If, like Ima, if you haven't been active in months and struggle with staying consistent, then it makes the most sense to start with a program that incorporates moderate amounts of activity into your lifestyle. Ima's greatest struggle is with time. One of her main objectives is to chisel out 40 minutes a day for herself. By planning ahead, Ima will be more successful at maintaining her running career.

Take the time to review your activity patterns. Be honest and realistic. There is no right or wrong response; your answer is merely one that will start you on the right path—a path that will lead you to greater things.

**Describe your past experience with running.**
- ☐ I have never run before in my life.
- ☐ I have run a little here and there but never consistently.
- ☐ I have run on and off for years.
- ☐ I run regularly three to five times per week.
- ☐ I run like Forrest Gump, across countries for miles and miles at a time.

**Ima Runner's answer:** I have tried several times to run. I tried to train for a 10-K last summer and wanted to finish it with my brother. Every time I run, I end up sore and don't enjoy it very much.

All too often we set our goals based on what we see around us rather than what we have to work with. I have witnessed this situation many times. Never having run before, Ima set herself up for failure by wanting to (1) run a 10-K and (2) run it with someone who's faster than she is.

I am by no means saying she couldn't have run that 10-K with her brother, but with that as her initial goal, she was likely to fail. Her body told her she was not ready to jump into a 10-K program, and she ended up injured and frustrated—an all-too-familiar pattern.

When selecting a running program for yourself, please beware if you are type A, or ambitious by nature. Type A characteristics are valuable in one sense—they probably motivated you to buy this book—but when it comes down to reality, you'll need to tame your overly ambitious goals and go conservative.

If you're training for your first running race, enjoy it! Set the goal to simply finish and enjoy every step. You will have plenty of time to improve and train for a time goal later on.

If you've already completed a 5-K or 10-K, want to improve your race time, and have been running regularly three to five times per week, start with one of the advanced running programs. You are ready to add a little more intensity and mileage to your running program and have the base to do so safely.

....................................................................

**How many days per week can you commit to training?**

- ☐ 5
- ☐ 3 or 4
- ☐ 2 or 3
- ☐ None or 1

**How many hours per week can you commit to training?**

- ☐ 8 or more
- ☐ 6 to 8
- ☐ 4 to 6
- ☐ Up to 4

**Ima Runner's answer:** I will commit to training 3 or 4 days and 2 to 3 hours per week.

. . . . . . . . . . . . . . . . . . . . . . . . . . . . . . . . . . . . . . . . . . . . . . . . . . . . . . . . . . . .

Commitment is key. You won't need to quit your job and sell your kids to run, but you will need to set aside time on a frequent basis. You may need to rearrange your daily activities and schedule. You may need to sit down with your family and explain that you will need "me time" to achieve your goals. You may even need to tell your coworkers why you aren't staying late.

You will need to commit a minimum of 2 to 3 hours per week to your program. It needs to be enough so your body remembers the activity week to week and will grow stronger workout to workout. Plus, the body that is in motion stays in motion. The more days you miss between workouts, the harder it will be to stick with a regular regimen. The goal is to create a regular habit, something your body looks forward to most days.

There's a lot of flexibility in your running program. You can move workouts and rest days to match your schedule and lifestyle. It is all a matter of working with the training principles of progression. Those will come later. For now, find the time and put it in your schedule.

. . . . . . . . . . . . . . . . . . . . . . . . . . . . . . . . . . . . . . . . . . . . . . . . . . . . . . . . . . . .

**What are the top two or three factors that motivate you to exercise?**

**Ima Runner's answer:** I am motivated by working out with friends and reaching for a specific goal.

. . . . . . . . . . . . . . . . . . . . . . . . . . . . . . . . . . . . . . . . . . . . . . . . . . . . . . . . . . . .

Identifying what motivates you will help keep the fire burning. Ima enjoys training with people and having a goal. Because of her schedule and family, she is better off scheduling runs with her friends.

The most important thing is to present your motivations in a realistic manner. For instance, Ima should train with buddies who have similar goals and are willing to train at the same pace. In fact, one of her girlfriends also wants to get in shape and learn to run. You may be motivated by the time for yourself or the fitness benefits. Whatever your motivations may be, list them at the top of your running program and read them often. These will be the fruits of your efforts and will keep you motivated to move forward.

**List your short- and long-term goals for running.**

> **Ima Runner's answers:** My short-term goal is to get back into a regular program of running 3 or 4 days a week without pain. My long-term goals are to lose 15 pounds and to run a 5-K race next summer.

Ima has done a great job of identifying her short- and long-term goals. Her first goal is to get back into running—without pain. That can be accomplished in 2 or 3 months. Her long-term goals are to lose weight and train to run a 5-K. She knows this may take longer and is excited about following a structured program for the 5-K.

**What will be your top challenges to following the training program?**

> **Ima Runner's answer:** I am crunched for time and have twin 3-year-olds to care for. Finding the time will be my greatest challenge.

Ima shares a common challenge with many people who commit to following a running program. Identifying things that may get in your way will help you avoid what we call the pitfalls of training. If time is precious, identify a program that makes sense for the time you can carve out. If you struggle to find someone to support you in your efforts, surround yourself with a new crowd of people who have similar goals. They're out there; all you need to do is find them and make the adjustments. Your life will change, as will your challenges, as you progress. Keep your focus and direction, and decrease the resistance. Your path will become more obvious and your goals more attainable.

## COACH JENNY'S TIPS AND TRICKS

✓ Use the Personal Inventory Form to gauge your current status and where you want to go.

✓ Select a running program that best suits your fitness level, experience, and goals. Starting with the right program will allow you to progress quickly.

✓ Realize that learning to run safely means starting with where you are rather than where you want to be.

✓ Never train through injury pain. Soreness is normal, but if you develop aches and pains, take a few days off. Try another activity that doesn't bother you or exacerbate your pain while your body heals. If the pain lingers longer than a few days, seek medical advice from a doctor specializing in sports medicine; ask the staff at your local running store for referrals.

# SECTION II
## TOOLS OF THE TRADE

# 5

# THE ANATOMY OF A RUN

Let's talk about your running workouts. A perfect run is like a fine meal. It flows seamlessly from the appetizer through the entrée and finishes with a tasty dessert. Although your runs will vary in distance and speed, the anatomy of the run will always flow from the warmup to running to the cooldown.

## APPETIZER: WARMUP

Every workout should begin with a proper warmup. Like an appetizer, the warmup prepares your body for what is to come. It gradually increases bloodflow to the working muscles, lungs, and heart. Similar to driving onto an expressway entrance ramp, you need to move slowly before you move quickly. Asking your body to go from 0 to 70 miles per hour in 2 seconds is asking for a very uncomfortable workout and quite possibly an injury. Your car runs better when it has a chance to warm up, and so does your body.

The warmup for your runs should start with a brisk walk for at least 5 minutes. Walking briskly will allow your body to gradually transfer oxygen-rich blood to the large moving muscles in your legs and arms. Start at a comfortable walking pace and increase your speed as you go. It may take patience, but you will definitely notice an easier transition to running if you devote a few short minutes to warming up.

Warming up is especially important when training first thing in the morning, when your muscles are cold and shortened from sleeping all night, or after a long day of sitting in an office chair. Your body will perform much more efficiently if you progress gradually from first gear to second and then third, rather than shocking it into the run.

Cross-training workouts should include a warmup as well. For instance, if you are cycling on your cross-training day, start with 5 minutes of easy-paced cycling to prepare your body for the session. It makes no difference whether you are walking, strength-training, or swimming. Start with a warmup at a slow pace, and you will be rewarded with a workout that will allow your body to function optimally.

Once your body is warmed up, move into an easy running pace and continue the workout. Save the flexibility exercises for after the workout, when your muscles are warm and more receptive to elongating.

Although you can stretch after the warmup, for a runner, this tends to be counterproductive because the body cools back down. We'll talk more about the importance of developing flexibility and when you should stretch in Chapter 13.

Just as you wouldn't eat the entrée before the appetizer, busting into your workout without an adequate warmup will run you the risk of having to slow down in the middle of your training session just to get through it. Devote a full 5 minutes to your warmup. If you need to shorten a workout due to time constraints, take a few minutes off the workout—the entrée—not the warmup.

## THE ENTRÉE: THE RUNNING WORKOUT

The main course of your training program is the time you spend walking or running for a specific time and intensity Every running workout has a specific purpose. Every workout is unique and a piece of the training puzzle.

The run-walk workout is the key ingredient for new or first-time runners. These workouts teach you how to run by mixing short intervals of running with fast-paced walking, or power walking. The run-walk method is the trendiest way to run these days because it is more forgiving on your body, allows you to run longer, and is very enjoyable. John loves run-walking so much that it's all he includes in his training. Jenny started her running career with run-walking and now uses the strategy for recovery runs.

The trick to run-walking is to avoid getting impatient with the walk. The walk breaks should not be actual breaks but, rather, fast-paced walking that keeps your heart rate up. If you were to plot your run on a graph, you'd see a gently rolling line representing the speed of your running and walking. Run at a conversational pace—a speed at which you can still talk. Walk at a brisk pace, or what we refer to as *power-walking speed*. There should be a very subtle transition from walk to run and run to walk.

You may start your running career with running and walking and progress to all running or, like John, decide to stick with run-walking. Either way, this valuable method will play a vital role in learning to run.

Some runs are short; some are long. The longer you run, the more you build up your endurance, or your ability to cover more miles over time. Building endurance is all about teaching your body to spend time on your feet. It should be done at a conversational or comfortable pace. The endurance workout is the longest of your runs and is scheduled for the weekend, when you probably have more time. Slow and steady is the quickest way to run farther and the optimal way to develop your aerobic-endurance system.

Speed workouts are included in the advanced training programs. These sessions are optimal only for runners who have a strong base of miles and have been running consistently without injury for at least 8 to 10 months. The speed workouts are similar to the run-walk workouts and include a variety of intervals of running and walking. The difference is that the run intervals are short and done at a high intensity, followed by easy-paced walking or running.

Speed workouts improve the body's ability to utilize oxygen more efficiently at the anaerobic level, which ultimately helps increase the speed of easy runs too. Some speed workouts include longer intervals at a comfortably hard pace; others call for short intervals at a harder pace. The variety is key in order to train all your gears to improve speed and performance.

As you get stronger, you will be able to run faster for longer periods of time with less recovery and leap tall buildings in a single bound. There is a place in your running career for playing with speed workouts, but it isn't during your first 6 to 8 months.

## HILL WORKOUTS

Hills are our friends. Hill workouts are a great way to build strength, stamina, and speed. Hills are like resistance training for a runner. They develop not only leg strength but cardiovascular stamina as well. And unless you live in the flatlands (Chicago) like us, you most likely will run hills in your daily runs or races.

You can run one hill several times or a bunch of hills along a course. Either way, don't fight the hill—be the hill. Aim to maintain your effort level going up by slowing down slightly and shortening your stride. That will give you enough energy at the top to relax into the downhill, extend your stride, and slightly lean into it and sail down. It is okay to push the uphill pace in training to get stronger, but make sure you are running hills efficiently in a race—slow on the way up and fast on the way down. The average of the two should equal the pace you were running at heading into the hill.

The training programs build gradually over time. This is the secret to running success. You can't build too quickly and expect to run well. Your body will tire and even burn out. It is best to build gradually week by week, allowing your body time to adapt to the demands of your training and then make further progress. You may notice the programs cut back every few weeks. This is what we call a spa week, or a time to chill on the progression and rest a little before you build again.

## STEAMED VEGETABLES: REST DAYS

Rest weeks are woven into the program. These are the vegetables that do you a lot of good, even if it doesn't seem that way. Every few weeks, the mileage will decrease after a phase of building, and you will most likely welcome this period with open arms. After building miles for a few weeks, a "cutback" week begins to look like vacation time. Use these cutback weeks wisely, and follow the mileage prescribed. Training harder or longer will only lead you down Overtraining Avenue. Use the time to catch up with family, stay busy with overdue projects or chores, or go to the movies. Just don't *add* mileage or intensity to your rest weeks.

For the purpose of this training program, rest is moving through your normal day in the absence of exercise. Rest does not mean lying on a couch all day eating bonbons. Think of rest days as training sleep. They're an integral part of the program and rejuvenate your body for the next workout.

Rest days are deceiving. At first you may think, *Great, I get to rest! What a treat.* Once committed fully to the training program, it becomes strangely harder and harder to rest. It is almost as if you are in a rhythm and don't want to stop. I've been witness to too many runners and walkers not resting and ultimately ending up injured. Rest is just as important as all of the other workouts. It allows your body to recover from the stress and impact of the training cycle. Your body can't go too long without adequate sleep, and it can't train optimally without rest days.

## SOME FRESHLY GROUND PEPPER? CROSS-TRAINING

Rest days follow longer or more intense workouts, while cross-training is strategically placed to balance your "moving muscles" to avoid overuse injuries. Consider cross-training a supplement to your running program. It helps balance the muscles that are commonly used while running. Like freshly ground pepper, cross-training spices things up for the running muscles that can get fatigued and tight, stride after stride. Cross-training activates various muscle groups, requiring them to move in different directions and, in most cases, with less impact on the body. Cycling, for example, is a favorite cross-training activity for runners, as it reduces the overall impact on the body but provides a great cardiovascular workout.

Cross-training is an important supplement to the training regimen—it brings out the flavor. I like to refer to it as *active rest* because it allows the running muscles a little nap time while activating the opposing muscles that are being neglected. Cross-training for runners includes anything except running—cycling, swimming, strength training, rowing, yoga, group exercise classes, or inline skating.

There are many ways to cross-train. The key is to select an activity you like. You will be more likely to enjoy the workout as it provides a mental and physical time-out from the structure and intensity of your running regimen.

## THE DESSERT MENU, PLEASE: THE COOLDOWN

Every good meal ends with dessert. The cooldown is the dessert of your training. Every workout, long or short, should end with a gradual slowing of pace and intensity—the reverse of the warmup.

Slowing down for 5 minutes allows your body to come back to reality by decreasing breathing and heart rate while bringing blood circulation to its resting route. Take 5 minutes, slow your pace, and relish your short-term achievements. It will not only aid in quick recovery but bring you back to earth with a smile on your face.

Once you're back to reality, take a few more minutes to stretch your fatigued muscles. Stretching postworkout is optimal, as the muscles are warm and therefore more pliable.

Similar to a good meal, a training program includes many

ingredients. Take the time to understand the value of each component because, as with stew, it's the blend that makes it all taste so good. The meal needs to start with an appetizer and finish with dessert. Anything less will equate to a fast-food meal, yielding low results and poor quality.

## ELBOWS OFF THE TABLE: GOOD RUNNING FORM

Everyone will vary in form. Each one of us has different feet, arms, and legs. Some of us are tall and some short. Some are genetically gifted and can run almost perfectly, while others will struggle to put one foot in front of the other. The idea is not to move like someone else but to run, walk, or crawl optimally for your mechanics.

Efficient form, whether walking or running, can make the difference in race time, performance, and risk of injury. Maintaining strong form throughout your training and racing will allow you to move faster and farther with less energy expenditure.

There's a reason your mother told you to keep your elbows off the table—and it's not just because she was nagging you about manners. Keeping your elbows off the table forces you to sit up straight instead of slumping over so you can more efficiently digest your food. Your form follows the same principle. The next time you work out, take a look at other walkers and runners around you and see what you think. What are the stronger, faster people doing with their arms, legs, and torsos? How does that differ from the slower people? Do some look awkward, while others appear to glide over the ground?

Proper form can save you precious time and energy, but if you are new to this concept, it won't change overnight. We mortals need to crawl before we walk and walk before we run. Focus on only a few aspects of your form each time you run. Otherwise, you may just drive yourself crazy trying to correct everything all at once.

The best way to improve your form is to perform a head-to-toe inventory once or twice when running. Making small adjustments can save a lot of energy and translate into more efficient times. The elements of a head-to-toe inventory:

- **Head** should be looking forward rather than down at the ground. Look down with only your eyes to check out the path; if you must move your head, do so, but then refocus on the horizon in front of you.

- **Shoulders** should be relaxed, with your elbows creating 90-degree angles, swinging freely like pendulums. Focus on pumping your elbows back and forth without crossing your arms across your navel.

- **Hands** are relaxed; pretend to hold on to a potato chip or something fragile. Clenched hands or fists waste energy.

- **Hips** should line up directly below your shoulders, rather than back, allowing your legs to swing through a greater range of motion and open up your gait.

- **Feet** should land lightly and quickly on the ground and under your hips. Pretend you are moving forward and there is a two-by-four 2 inches above your head. Land on the middle portion of your foot and push through to the toes, propelling your body forward rather than up and down.

Focus on quick turnover or strides. Like climbing stairs, if you take shorter steps one at a time, your turnover is faster, and you move up more quickly using less energy than if you climb three stairs at a time. Most new runners try to cover too much ground stride for stride. A good test to see if you are overstriding is to count the number of strides (steps) on one foot while running for 1 minute. If you are in the range of 88 to 92 strides on one foot within 1 minute, you are in the efficient zone. If you are much less, focus on shortening your stride and speeding your turnover. The result will be faster running with less impact on the body and reduced risk of injury. It may feel weird at first, but you're learning a new skill, and it will take time for your body and mind to adapt.

## THE RESTAURANT: RUNNING SURFACES

The variety of running surfaces is like your choice of restaurants. Some are convenient but not necessarily good for you. Others may be harder to find but a lot better for your muscles, tendons, and joints.

Concrete sidewalks are like fast-food restaurants: all over the place and convenient but very hard on your body. The sidewalk keeps you safe from traffic and is predictable, but it is the hardest of all running terrains because it puts tremendous stress on the body. We are not fans of running on concrete, but we do it when we have to.

Asphalt is a little more forgiving on the body than concrete and equally as convenient. Although still hard on the body, asphalt is preferable to concrete, and it's the most common outdoor running surface for mortal runners.

Dirt paths and trails are Jenny's favorites. Trails are excellent surfaces for runners because they are soft and easy on the body. Some old railroad routes are very predictable, while others are akin to the Yellow Brick Road, with exposed tree roots, rocks, and flying monkeys. Trails like these are mentally consuming and are great for your training because every step is different. Additionally, you recruit a variety of muscles rather than the same ones over and over again.

Most tracks these days are made of synthetic materials designed to absorb shock. The measured distance lets you always know where you are and provides safety if you are running alone.

Grass is very soft and can be a great place to train, especially if you are a trail runner or looking to race in an off-road event. However, remember to be cautious when running on grass, as there can be many holes and lumps.

One of Jenny's favorite runs is along South Carolina's Myrtle Beach. Running on flat and firm sand is easy on the body and a treat for most runners. Avoid uneven or soft sand, which places a lot of stress on the body and can lead to a muscle injury.

Treadmills are convenient, easy to use, and a great way to control your speed and pace. Treadmills are made to absorb shock and do so better than most running surfaces. You can also vary terrain and workouts with the touch of a button. We run on treadmills, especially in the winter months, when the ground is icy and unpredictable. Jenny has trained for the Eco-Challenge on a treadmill and John for the Pikes Peak Marathon. How else can flatlanders get a great hill workout in?

Treadmill running is easier on the joints and easier in intensity too. Running outdoors is more challenging due to the elements like wind and rolling terrain. When you take your workout outside, you propel yourself forward versus keeping up with the tread, making your energy expenditure slightly lower on the treadmill. The experts say to run at a 2 percent grade on the treadmill to equate to outdoor running, but Coach Jenny disagrees. Running at a constant incline can create a host of overuse injuries. If you are just learning to run, don't worry about the difference; just get on there and go at the appropriate pace. If you are seasoned, vary the intensity by running a rolling course or increasing the speed slightly. It will all come out in the wash, and you won't end up with an injury.

A good adventure-racing friend once taught us that three is two,

two is one, and one is none—meaning, having more than one piece of gear will better prepare you for the road ahead. This is also true with running routes. Running three or four different routes that vary in terrain and difficulty will help you avoid boredom and injury. Variety is the spice of a runner's life. We love running on the lakefront path in Chicago, but we have the most fun when we venture off the beaten path and run our own routes. Alternate your running routes, and you will use different muscles, run at varying intensities, and prevent boredom.

## COACH JENNY'S TIPS AND TRICKS

✓ Start every workout with a warmup. It is the key component to preparing your body safely for the run ahead.

✓ Run three or four routes rather than just one. Alternating treadmill training with outdoor training is a great way to mix things up.

✓ First-time runners: Stick with easy-paced running and focus on building your base. You will soon run farther and even a little faster—all in due time.

✓ Seasoned runners: Sprinkle in faster-paced speed workouts to improve performance and efficiency.

✓ Make small changes over time. Good form means something different for everyone. Awareness is the first step to running more efficiently.

✓ Finish every workout with a gradual cooldown. It brings your body back to reality, aids in a more efficient recovery, and avoids the shock of stopping abruptly.

# 6

# FOUNDATIONS OF FITNESS

## PENGUIN PEARLS OF WISDOM

*My early training was equal parts sheer lunacy and pure stupidity. I foolishly believed that tearing my body down was the way to build my body up.*

After years of abusing our bodies with alcohol, nicotine, overeating, or overworking, it's easy to switch to abusing our bodies with too much exercise.

It's easy to start punishing the very bodies we had abused in the first place by expecting too much, demanding too much, and taking on too much.

First and foremost, an athlete has to come to terms with what his or her body can and cannot do, and then learn to work within those limitations.

**POP QUIZ: When does the training effect occur?**

A. When you're training

B. When you're resting

C. None of the above

D. All of the above

If you guessed A, then you are in the right place, because you're wrong, and we can help you.

If you guessed C or D, then, well, we can still help you, but it's not going to be easy.

If you guessed B, then you're on your way to becoming an athlete—or you're just a good guesser.

For many new athletes, the tired old adage "No pain, no gain" still seems to be stuck in their heads. When we start introducing new runners to our training programs, they often worry that the training seems too easy. They wonder how anything that feels so comfortable can be doing them any good.

In most cases, the misunderstanding comes from a lack of knowledge about how the body—your body, my body, every body—really works. It's not nearly the mystery that you think it is. In fact, once you understand some of the basics, it's pretty simple.

It's all about the systems in the body and the way they react to increased stress. The systems are related to each other but are not identical. They can work in harmony, but only if each is given time to adjust to the new demands being placed on them.

Our bodies, at least the parts that we're going to focus on, consist of three main systems: the *aerobic* system (heart and lungs), the *muscular* system (the muscles), and the *skeletal* system (bones, joints, tendons, etc.). As runners, we are asking each of these systems to adapt to new stresses. The key to success is knowing how, when, and why the systems change.

We tend to take our aerobic system for granted because it is there working away all the time. Very few of us spend any time at all thinking about our hearts and lungs. We count on them to be there for us, and we only pay attention to them if something goes wrong. It's a good thing that they do work without any input from us; if we had to remember to breathe or pump blood, most of us wouldn't last a week.

Remember back to your junior high school health class. There was that chart that showed how oxygen was brought into the lungs through the nose and then got into the bloodstream and was pumped into the body by the heart. What keeps your body going is that constant flow of oxygen circulating through your blood. That's true as you sit there and read this, and it's true as you begin to transform yourself into an athlete.

As you begin to move more—as you begin to walk or run (or cycle or perform any kind of activity that places a demand on your heart for more oxygen)—your heart reacts almost immediately to that new demand. It has to. It has to in order to keep you alive.

If, like many people, you take off on your first run and bolt down the street as fast as you can, your heart goes into panic mode. Your lungs are demanding oxygen, and your heart just can't keep up. So your heart does the only thing it knows how to do in that situation: It shuts your body down.

If, as we are suggesting, you start to move a little more, a little at a time, your heart can meet those new incremental demands and won't shut down.

The most amazing part is how quickly your aerobic system adapts to new demands. By asking for small increases in bloodflow, by walking or running at a comfortable pace for a small amount of time, you can begin to see measurable improvement in your aerobic system in as little as 3 weeks.

Three weeks—because your aerobic system is so highly developed, it can make those adaptations almost immediately. This explains why after just a few weeks of being active, almost everybody starts to feel better. Their hearts beat better, their lungs work better, and life is good.

That's when the problems begin.

Your muscular system is not as efficient as your aerobic system. It does not make the adaptation to the new stress caused by activity in the same way and in the same amount of time as your aerobic system. Here's an example of how—too often—a person starts an exercise routine and why it is doomed to failure.

**Monday: Run 3 miles.** Our new runner is all fired up about getting into shape. His brother-in-law (who used to be a runner until he injured himself) tells him that he should be able to run 3 miles at a 7-minute-per-mile pace, so that's what he tries to do. Of course, he can't. He goes out too fast and his muscles get tired, but he keeps pushing and finishes the 3 miles exhausted and discouraged.

**Tuesday: Run 3 miles.** Not wanting to seem undisciplined and still excited about getting into shape, he tries running 3 miles again. This time, though, his muscles are tired from Monday, so it's even harder to run. He stumbles forward and manages to run-walk the 3 miles, but he notices a little ache in his knee.

**Wednesday: Run 3 miles.** He is determined. Sure, he's tired. Sure, his knee hurts, but hey—no pain, no gain. So he takes on the run again. This time though, his muscles are really tired and sore. His knee is really bothering him. But he refuses to quit and manages to walk and jog the 3 miles.

**Thursday: Run 3 miles.** He is in agony. The knee that hurt a little yesterday is killing him today. There's a funny pain on the outside of the other knee, his hips hurt, and his muscles are just about shot. But he is determined. So he pushes himself out the door, only to have to stop about 100 yards into the run because he can barely walk. He turns around and goes back into the house, totally discouraged.

**Friday: Call brother-in-law—can't be a runner because of bad knees.** Sound familiar? It might if you've ever tried to start a running program before. And make no mistake, that's exactly how we started and failed at becoming runners ourselves. But it doesn't have to be that way.

Our muscles are structured in layers. The layer that we use most of the time, what we call our Monday muscles, is in relatively good shape. So, when we go out for that first run or walk, most of the effort is eaten up by the Monday muscles.

On Tuesday, our Monday muscles are still tired, so they send out a call for the next layer of muscle tissue. The problem is, this layer of muscle hasn't been used much recently and isn't in the kind of shape that the Monday muscles are in. So the Tuesday muscles tire out more quickly than the Monday muscles do, and the run is much more difficult.

Come Wednesday, the Monday *and* Tuesday muscles are wasted, so the call goes out for the next layer of muscle. But this layer hasn't been called on since you were 12 years old! This layer is in terrible condition and has no stamina or endurance at all. With no muscle strength left, the joints don't have any support, and the stress on them begins to make them ache.

By Thursday, there are no muscles left at all, except those that you haven't used since you were crawling across the floor as a baby. These muscles are nearly worthless to you. The joints are totally unprotected from the stress and begin to break down.

Friday: You're done.

Make sense?

The only way—the *only* way—to get the muscle adaptation you need is by giving those muscles time to rest and recover. For the typical adult, that means about 48 hours of rest in between runs. During that period, your Monday muscles put out a call to the heart and lungs and explain that they need more oxygen in order to heal themselves. The veins and arteries get involved in the action and start building additional capillaries to carry that extra blood into the muscles.

The Monday muscles also start talking to the Tuesday muscles and tell them to get off their dead butts and get involved in this process. The Tuesday muscles are not all that excited, but they answer the call.

With a little rest, your Monday muscles can carry you nearly as far as they did the first time, and the call to the Tuesday muscles is only for a little support, not to completely take over. In the meantime, your joints are protected by the strongest muscles you have available and are not as likely to ache!

As your running time and distance increase, you'll begin to engage more and more muscle fibers, until you reach the point where all the muscles are engaged in helping you become a better runner.

One small problem: While your aerobic system can achieve one cycle of measurable improvement in 3 to 6 weeks, your muscular system achieves one cycle of measurable improvement in 6 to 12 weeks. What that means is that for some new runners, the aerobic system can progress two to four times faster than their muscular system.

This time difference in cycles of improvement or, more precisely, the lack of understanding about this difference is why so many people find themselves with muscle soreness 3 to 4 weeks into an exercise or running program. What happens is that their heart and lungs start feeling better right away. In just a few weeks, these new runners decide they should be able to run farther or faster just because they feel so much better aerobically.

But the body doesn't work that way. You have to be patient. You have to be smart. You have to know that your muscles are getting fitter at a much more gradual pace than your heart and lungs are. And you have to pace yourself.

And as if *that* wasn't enough to worry about, you've got to consider your skeletal system. Your skeletal system goes through one complete cycle of measurable improvement in 6 to 12 months.

Six to 12 *months*.

That means your aerobic system is changing every 3 to 4 weeks, and your muscles are changing every 6 to 12 weeks, but your joints and tendons won't—and can't—change except every 6 to 12 months. Your aerobic system could experience 12 improvement cycles, and your muscles could experience four or five, for every *one* improvement cycle of your skeletal system.

That is why people so often begin to experience joint pain after just a few months of running. It's not hard to understand now, is it? Their hearts and lungs are feeling better than ever and their muscles are starting to feel great, so they push themselves to go farther and faster before their joints and tendons are ready.

The simplest way to understand this is to think of the amount of blood going to each of these systems: Lots of blood in the heart and lungs—fast improvement. Less blood in the muscles—slower improvement. Nearly no blood in the joints and tendons—very slow improvement.

Just knowing and understanding these three systems and how they work, both independently and cooperatively, can make the difference between becoming a lifelong athlete and being injured.

And take it from us, being active is better than being injured.

## COACH JENNY'S TIPS AND TRICKS

✓ Progress gradually, and avoid pushing yourself too much too soon. Rome wasn't built in a day. It takes time for your muscles, tendons, and ligaments to adapt to the impact of running.

✓ Listen to your body for signs of overtraining: aches and pains that don't go away, irritability, being crabbier than normal, loss of appetite, and insomnia. If you show signs of overtraining, back off your training and rest a few days.

✓ If you are coming to running from another sport or activity, be aware of the differences in impact forces. It is wise to be conservative with distance and speed even if running seems easy. Let your skeletal system adapt.

✓ Be smart; run wisely. It's easy to head out and run too far too fast. Anyone can do that. It takes discipline to run wisely and at the right effort level.

✓ Slow down, and you will speed the progression of your running. Running shouldn't be painful; challenging, yes, but if you are in pain, you are going too hard.

# 7

# ELEMENTS OF EFFORT

All righty then! If you've made it this far, there's a pretty good chance that you're interested in learning to run, or getting fit, or losing weight, or *something*. That, or you just have way too much time on your hands.

We've tried everything we can think of to make all of this fun and interesting, but the truth is—it isn't all that thrilling. It is, kinda, in the way that finding out how your intestines process food is interesting, but it's not the sort of topic that makes you run out and buy a book.

That's why we waited until Chapter 7.

That might be unfair. There may be some readers who get into the nitty-gritty stuff. You may be the kind of person who actually understands what the difference is between *ram* and *rom* on your computer or why your car gets better gas mileage with a 3.87 rear end ratio than a 3.97. If that's you, hold on tight, because you're going to love the next few pages.

If you're like most people, though, and you just want to know where the on-off button is on your computer or where to put gas into your car, then this might require a little patience and discipline on your part.

Simply put, you need to understand what kinds of effort there are, how your body reacts to effort, why your body reacts the way it does, how that reaction affects your perception of that effort, and what to do about it once you know. Stay with me.

At the center of all of this is your heart. Your heart is nothing more than this big-energy fire-and-rescue station for your body. It could not care less what kind of effort you're making. It will not demand or require you to do anything. It is designed only to respond to the demands being placed on it.

The first demand is to keep you alive. That's the lowest point of demand that you can make. The number that people associate with it is called your *resting heart rate.*

For most people, the resting heart rate is at its lowest in the morning. But if you're the kind of person who wakes up in a state of near panic because of everything you've got to do that day, chances are your resting heart rate will not be low in the morning.

If you're the kind of person who winds down and mellows out (*without* the use of alcohol or drugs!) in the evening, then your resting heart rate will likely be lower at night just before you go to sleep.

Why should you care about your resting heart rate? Because it is the single most accurate measure of your current level of fitness and the best measure of your increasing level of fitness.

If, for example, you measure your heart rate tonight and it is 72 beats per minute, that means nothing except that your heart has to beat 72 times per minute just to keep you alive. If you call your friend (who has also bought the book and is reading it with you) and her resting heart rate is 68, that means only that on that day her heart had to beat 68 times per minute to keep her alive.

If you were to perform some Dr. Frankenstein-like experiment and switch hearts, yours might still beat more in her body than in yours, or it might beat more slowly. But in any case, it doesn't matter. Lower, within reason, doesn't mean better.

The other number that's good to know, but you probably don't and won't, is your *maximum heart rate*. This is the fastest your heart can beat under any given circumstance. It doesn't matter if you're running or walking, falling out of an airplane, or falling in love—your maximum heart rate is a fixed number. Your max is your max.

And, just like your resting heart rate, your max is pretty much unique to you. It is based on gender and age and your physical makeup—but it has nothing to do with your level of fitness. You cannot increase your maximum heart rate through exercise.

Unlike your resting heart rate, which you can control to a certain extent, your max heart rate is pretty well set at birth and gets lower and lower with every passing year. You can control the rate of descent somewhat, but you can't stop your max from getting lower over time.

None of the formulas given for calculating your maximum heart rate based on your age are anywhere close to accurate. The old 220 (for men) or 226 (for women) minus your age is notorious for being wrong. The most accurate formula is 205 minus one-half your age. So, for a 40-year-old person, the max calculates to 185.

It calculates to 185, but it may not *be* 185. This is because we all have different heart sizes and heart rates, and using one formula calculates properly for just a very small percentage of people. We only mention it because we know you're going to try to find out what yours is no matter what we say! And if you decide you must know your actual maximum heart rate, find a high-quality sports medicine facility that will strap you up and let you go at it. Again, you don't need to do this, but if you absolutely have to know that number, get it done right.

Knowing your maximum heart rate gives you an accurate number from which to determine your training heart rate zones. This is key information if you plan to keep tabs on your effort in training with a heart rate monitor. Although using one is not required, Coach Jenny highly recommends it. There are many monitors now that are easy to use and give you instant feedback about how hard your body is working. It takes all the guessing out of training at the correct effort level. (More on heart rate monitors in Chapter 16.)

The number that we care about in terms of effort is the difference between your maximum heart rate (real or calculated) and your resting heart rate. That number is called your *cardiac reserve*: the amount of "heart" that you have to work with as an athlete. Your resting heart rate is what your body needs to stay alive. Your max is your max. What's left for *you* is the cardiac reserve.

Now, some of you may have skipped ahead in your thinking: *If I can lower my resting heart rate by becoming more fit, then even though I can't change my maximum heart rate, I can increase my cardiac reserve!* If you figured that out by yourself, give yourself an A and go to the head of the class.

For the math-impaired (like us), we'll explain: Your resting heart rate is a measure of your fitness. As you get fitter, that number goes down. Even with your max staying the same, your cardiac reserve increases because your resting heart rate gets lower faster than your maximum heart rate does. Got it?

Our 40-year-old friend has a current resting heart rate of 85 and a calculated maximum heart rate of 185. Her cardiac reserve is 100 beats. She starts on a walk-run program, and after a few months, her resting heart rate is down to 75, which means her cardiac reserve is now 110 beats. That's a 10 percent increase in accessible cardiac energy, which is a pretty good return on the investment.

Why do you care? Because when you're talking about effort—real effort versus perceived effort, getting fit and building a healthier heart, and greater cardiac efficiency delivering blood to the muscles in response to demand based on effort—you're really talking about the increase in your cardiac reserve.

Just a couple of more things, and we'll move on.

We all have an *anaerobic threshold*: the point at which the muscles start using more oxygen than the body can supply. This is also the point at which muscles can no longer "exhaust" the toxic buildup that results from muscle demand and use. This exhaust is called *lactic acid*, and it is the by-product of the muscles firing.

If you've ever seen a runner "locking up" at the end of a race, you know what we're talking about. You'll see it most often at the end of a final sprint in a 5-K, when a runner has just gone beyond that threshold, and there's nothing he can do. His legs fill with the toxic lactic acid, and he comes screeching to a halt.

The funny thing about the anaerobic threshold is that it is, indeed, a threshold. It's a line . . . a number . . . an exact point at which your body goes anaerobic. Below that line, life is good. Above that line, there's trouble in the making.

You've actually got to be in pretty decent shape to experience this anaerobic threshold. This is not what happens the first time you try to sprint down your driveway and find yourself bent over and gasping for air. That isn't your anaerobic threshold. That's just how out of shape you are.

Where most of us want to be most of the time is in our *aerobic zone*. *Aerobic* simply means "in the presence of oxygen." What that means to us as athletes is that we want to be exercising, running, walking, or whatever at a level of effort that is low enough that our hearts can deliver the amount of oxygenated blood our muscles are demanding.

Unlike the anaerobic threshold, which is a line and very narrow, our aerobic zone is a zone and quite wide—everything in between our resting heart rate and our anaerobic threshold.

Okay, you smarty-pants. I can see you doing the math already. You're thinking that your aerobic zone is also increased by lowering your resting heart rate. But it's not quite that simple.

For most people, the anaerobic threshold is at about 85 percent of maximum heart rate, but you can't just multiply the max by 0.85 to find that out. You've got to use the cardiac reserve, and then add back the resting heart rate.

Back to our 40-year-old. She starts with a cardiac reserve of 100. Eighty-five percent of 100 is 85; that plus her resting heart rate of 85 beats per minute makes her effective anaerobic threshold 170.

As she gets fit, her cardiac reserve becomes 110. Eight-five percent of 110 is 93; adding back her new resting heart rate of 75 makes her new anaerobic threshold—wait—168! Aha! See, that's why you don't want to get ahead of us.

You hear all this chatter about raising your anaerobic threshold, but it just isn't true. You can't. You *can* get better at knowing exactly where your anaerobic threshold is, what it feels like when you approach it, and what it feels like to stay right on the edge, but you're not going to make it higher.

"Why do I care about this?" we hear you asking. Because some of you will want to get faster, and you think you'll get faster by working harder or pushing yourself further and willing your body to withstand more pain. You won't. You'll get faster by getting more efficient and learning how to place less demand on your heart at a given pace.

Which brings us to the only four words you really need to know to get started and improve on your training. These are the essential elements of every training program and the ones we will continue to refer to throughout this book. They are:

Frequency—Intensity—Duration—Mode

*Frequency* means how often. How often are you going to exercise? How often are you going to put stress on some particular element of your physiology? How many days per week? How much stress? How much recovery?

*Intensity* refers to how much demand is being placed on the various systems. An intense cardio workout may not be an intense skeletal workout and vice versa.

*Duration* is how long you are going to do whatever it is that you're doing.

*Mode* means simply: What the heck are you doing? Running, walking, cycling, swimming, chasing your dog?

Frequency and mode seem pretty self-explanatory. Your frequency is likely to be less early on because you will need more rest and recovery time. As we've explained, you can't jump into a 6-day-a-week training program if you've been inactive most of your life.

The decision on frequency is a highly individual one, based in part on your general state of fitness, goals, age, lifestyle, rate of recovery, etc. The key is to match the frequency with your current activity program. If you are inactive, start conservatively with three or four times per week. If you are looking to follow the Weight Loss

Program, you'll notice the frequency is higher and the duration or time is lower. It is more important in that program to rev up your metabolism more frequently than to build your mileage.

Mode is also a highly personal decision. We are runners first and foremost, but we are not runners exclusively. We like to bicycle. We like to kayak. We like to hike. In fact, we like almost any activity that gets us moving. You may find that running or walking twice a week is the most your body can handle safely. So be it. Your aerobic system doesn't care. You may need to mix and match modes to allow your muscular and skeletal systems to catch up with your heart and lungs.

The two key concepts are intensity and duration. And they can't be separated from one another; they are inextricably linked now and forever. Whether this is your first week or if you've been an athlete all of your life, intensity and duration are inversely proportional.

The following are the only three rules in our training programs.

1. The higher the intensity, the shorter the duration.

2. The longer the duration, the lower the intensity.

3. You can't change rules 1 and 2.

There is no escaping these rules. You can try, but it won't work. If you want an intense workout, it has to be short and sweet. If you want a long workout, it's got to be at a comfortable level of effort.

We are amazed at how difficult it is for some new runners to understand the basics of inversely proportional effort and intensity. They get it in their minds that if running hard for a little bit is good, then running hard for a long time is better. It isn't.

All of this is important to understand if you want to be successful. We know that it works. We've seen thousands of people's lives changed merely by understanding how their bodies work.

## COACH JENNY'S TIPS AND TRICKS

✓ If you are a new runner, all your runs should be in the "aerobic," or comfortable, zone. This allows your cardiovascular and musculoskeletal systems time to adapt to the training.

✓ Use a system to monitor your intensity. Heart rate monitors or our i-Rate Scale of perceived effort (explained in the training programs in the Appendix) are two great ways to monitor effort levels.

✓ Use the right gear or speed. Most of the time, you will use gears one and two for easy-paced training. For faster-paced runs, use gears three and four, and when approaching the finish line of a race, go to gear five. Avoid relying on third and fourth gears for all your training. It may feel good to train hard, but eventually the demands of overtraining will take their toll.

✓ As a new runner, you should alternate run days with cross-training or rest days. The body will have time to recover, get stronger, and run farther and faster. Avoid trying to crank up the frequency for 6 to 8 months, when you'll have a sound base of regular running under your belt.

✓ The fun factor goes down the faster you run. The faster you go, the harder it is, the crabbier you get, and the less you want to run again. The key to developing a continuous running program is to alternate the frequency of running with cross-training and rest, and keep the intensity comfortable and the duration short.

✓ Use the training programs in our book. They are structured to safely progress week to week and are consecutive, so you can start with one and build to another program.

# 8

# WINNING THE MENTAL GAME

As a young man, I had visions of becoming a racquetball player. I got all the equipment, bought the shoes, signed out the court, and got ready to go.

A good friend agreed to teach me the game. His instructions were simple: "Be the ball." Be the ball? I had no idea what that meant. I couldn't even figure out how to hit the ball, let alone *be* the ball.

After a few weeks, though, the truth of what he said became clearer. As I focused less on where I was and what I was going to do, and more on where the ball was and what *it* was going to do, I suddenly found myself in a position to hit the ball more often. I still couldn't hit it where I wanted it to go, but at least I was beginning to get a sense of how the ball thought and acted and reacted to the game.

When I started running, I was trying to be a runner. I tried to control every aspect of what I was doing. The more I read about running, the more control I tried to exert on every aspect of my running.

I tried to run tall. I tried to run like I was being pulled on a string. I tried to run like there was a rubber band tied around my chest and pulling me forward. I tried to run like I was running on hot coals. I tried it all.

Eventually, I came to learn that the runner I wanted to be was inside my head. The runner that I was trying to become was already there in my mind, in my imagination. All I needed to do was to try to close the gap between what I imagined I could be and what I actually was.

I imagined myself running effortlessly. I imagined myself looking like Ironman champion Mark Allen. I imagined myself running with a purpose, with a steady rhythm.

When I was able to stop looking at myself from the outside—when I stopped looking at the awful gait, the awkward form, the painfully slow pace, and the complete lack of finesse—I started to look like a runner.

When I looked at myself from the inside out—when I listened to my heart beating; when I listened to my lungs working; when I listened to the sound of my feet hitting the ground, step after step, relentlessly carrying me forward—I started to feel like a runner.

I discovered for myself what most experienced runners already knew: Ninety percent of running is—to paraphrase Yogi Berra—75 percent mental.

What prevented me from being a runner in the first place was that I couldn't imagine myself as a runner. And if you can't imagine it, you can't do it. Once I imagined myself running, I was already on my way to becoming a runner.

What prevented me from running a 10-K or marathon or any other distance was that I couldn't imagine myself doing it. It wasn't my body that was keeping me from achieving my dreams; it was my imagination.

Even as the changes in my body were becoming more obvious, even after the weight had started to come off and I was running on a regular basis, I was still imagining myself as I used to be, not as I was.

We have training programs to take our bodies slowly but surely to greater distances and faster paces. We have guidelines on how much to run, how far, how fast, and how often. But sometimes our bodies will get weeks and months ahead of our imaginations.

If you are running, you are a runner. If you are running, you have a right to imagine yourself running the way you want. If you are running, you have the privilege of thinking like a runner.

When I was a musician, I encountered the world as a musician. I saw, heard, and experienced the world as a musician. I heard the melodies of life. I heard the harmony and discord around me. I heard the world as a symphony in which I was playing my small part.

Now I encounter the world as an athlete and a runner. I see and experience the world as a series of struggles and recovery. I take my running and apply it to my life. I know that there are good days and bad days. I know that there are days when easy is hard and hard is easy.

I think like a runner even when I'm not running. I have a runner's mind no matter what I'm doing.

I see effort, any effort, as a necessary element of growth. I see that I need a pattern of stress and recovery in order to get stronger. I experience my body as a tool to help me achieve my goals, not simply as a vessel in which I have to live my life.

I have become the shoe. I am traveling the road without thought and without concern. I am moving forward one step at a time. The last step is behind me; I can't change it. The next step is yet to come; I am not there yet.

I am only this one step. I am only this one moment, one instant. It is all that I can ever imagine myself being.

Jenny's journey through 10 days in the jungles of Borneo and Fiji in the Eco-Challenge expedition races had an incredible effect on her mental game. In her first attempt, she stood at the starting line like a deer in the headlights with competitors from all over the world, thinking, *Okay, only 10 days to go.* Very quickly, she realized that wasn't a good mental plan and began to break down the distance to smaller, more digestible pieces. Days turned into minutes and checkpoints. She mentally took herself through the race from checkpoint to checkpoint rather than trying to digest the whole race all at once. Suddenly, she was racing and feeling positive about the smaller goals she reached, which allowed her and her team to ultimately finish the race.

*How can I do this? How is my body going to run a 5-K race if I can't even get down my street?* These are real questions that can float around in our heads. Most people think them—and if they don't, they are worried about something else.

How do you get rid of that little voice that whispers in your ear, *Stop, you can't do this; just hang up your shoes and go to Starbucks—you're doomed?*

Although it may seem that physical training is the key to successful running, it is mental fitness that is the foundation that supports everything you do. As with the physical, mental fitness grows through experience and time. Your mind is the control room for your body. If the guys in the tower are transmitting negative signals, imagine what will happen to your run.

If, however, you have an intervention with the guys in the tower and tell them there is a paradigm shift and we need to send out positive signals, you will run and smile, and your efforts will be much easier. If you have a run-in with a negative thought during your run or a worry about finishing, simply take a deep breath and focus on all the good things you've done thus far.

Relax . . . If you are having a rough day, slow your pace and mentally focus on taking it one step at a time. If you are having a great day, take notes on your thoughts during the workout. Most runs can be more joyful if you quiet the voices and tune in to what is going on around you.

How will you reach your goal if it seems daunting? A good adventure racing friend of ours once told Jenny, "You can't eat an elephant in one bite, but you can eat it one bite at a time."

Only think about the next few minutes or the mile ahead. Surrender to the fact that you will be out there for 30 minutes, 1 hour, or however long it will take you, and then develop a mental plan with shorter goals to get through it.

If you are run-walking, you already have a great mental plan. If you are running 5 minutes and walking 1 minute, all you have to do is focus on the next 5 minutes of running.

Take care of yourself nutritionally. If you get low on blood sugar, your mind will be the first to fade, and you will slip into what we call the Bite Me Zone. That is an invitation to negative thoughts. Avoid skipping meals, and keep your blood sugar levels stable all day.

If things get tough, think about how you want to feel after the run or race is over. Do you want to feel proud and excited about what you've just accomplished or sad about the outcome? In the expedition races I've run, I've thought about how things could always be worse. I could be running up a mountain or in sand or not feeling well, or I could have just sat on a cactus while trying to go to the bathroom. It can always be worse. Have faith in your training and in yourself. Believe you can do it. As scary as it can be, surrender to the unknown and enjoy every step you take. The training is your journey, and the races are the celebrations!

You are what you think. We all respond differently to the same scenario. John may get anxious about a longer run, and I sometimes get fearful of a race. Our thoughts and emotions are based on our experience and self-talk or how we feel about ourselves.

Research indicates that athletes who perform optimally maintain a positive outlook. When we hold positive beliefs about ourselves, we will get positive outcomes: *I am going to run 30 minutes today and finish the best I can.*

On the other hand, if we think negative thoughts, we tend to have more negative experiences: *I'm doomed. I am never going to finish this run today.* The key is that you have the power to change your thinking process.

Jenny heads out for a 40-minute run after a long day. She is tired, feels crabbier than normal, and has little motivation. She can go into the run and continue to think negatively, *or* she can get out there, perhaps lower her expectations of the workout, and think about how much better she will feel when it's over. It's all about how we phrase things. Generally, the more positively we think, the better life feels. The more negatively we think, the more we struggle.

It is also fair to mention that having flexibility is important in a runner's life. Let's say you decide to run a 5-K race. You've been training all season and are ready to go. You've got your shoes and apparel, and you've trained your body and mind for the challenge. The gun goes off, it starts to rain, and your motivation disappears.

Because you're a first-timer, this could be enough outside stimulus to really throw you off your mental game. However, you have trained your mind to be flexible so you can deal with each obstacle as it comes your way. This is also a very important skill to use in everyday life. How many days are perfect?

## COACH JENNY'S TIPS AND TRICKS

✓ Break what seem to be overwhelming challenges into smaller, more digestible pieces. If it is a 30-minute run, think about the first 5 minutes or a location on your running course and then the next 5 minutes or another location. Starting with a 5-minute goal is much more feasible than thinking about the whole 30 minutes all at once.

✓ You are what you think. Train your mind to work with your body. It is a 50/50 partnership, and you will go farther with both fully on board.

✓ Be flexible mentally as well as physically. You may need to alter your workout due to fatigue or your race strategy due to weather. Go with what the run brings. You never know; you just may enjoy the run that starts off feeling awful.

✓ On days when your motivation is low, trick yourself into a run. Think about how you feel if you don't run versus when you do. Put on your running shoes and clothes. In most cases, that's enough to kick-start your enthusiasm. Head out on a new course or look at your running log. Getting your mind stimulated and excited about running in most cases will also motivate your body.

✓ Make detailed notes in your log about how you feel (happy, nervous, exhilarated, pumped) after workouts. It's fun to go back and review when you were nervous about 30-minute runs and see how far you've come.

✓ Focus on your goals, and stay realistic. Comparing yourself to someone who runs faster or farther is a great way to diminish your accomplishments and throw you into a negative mental state.

✓ Reward yourself for your accomplishments. Savor the positive energy of reaching a goal.

✓ Avoid trying to control what's out of your control—weather, late start, lack of sleep, race course, people...You waste precious mental energy and suck the life out of your run. Accept the fact that you can't control those factors, and think about ways you will deal with them before they happen.

✓ See yourself running. Visualize the race course or the next run. Consider it mental rehearsal and a great way to prepare your mind for the next event.

# SECTION III

## BECOMING A RUNNER

# 9

# YOUR FIRST WEEK

## PENGUIN PEARLS OF WISDOM

*Every run has the potential to transform us from who we are to the person we're becoming. Every step on every run could be the one that begins our metamorphosis from who we've always been to what we've always wanted to be.*

It's easy to confuse excitement with fear. It's easy to misunderstand what you're feeling on those first few days.

The power that has driven humans since the beginning of time is alive in your soul. The need to reach beyond yourself is burning inside of you.

Release yourself from your self-imposed limitations. Let your body guide you to a world where nothing seems impossible.

Oh boy, oh boy, oh boy! Isn't this exciting? It's like the first week of school. You're kinda scared but kinda excited all at once. You know it's going to be fun, you know you're going to learn some things, but you're not really sure what's coming next.

Before we hop on the bus, we need to get a few supplies. We need to make sure we've got our pens and pencils, our Elmer's Glue and notebooks. Without the right tools, we'd be lost at school. The same is true with running.

The first thing we want you to do is sit down; take off your shoes and socks; and take a good, long, honest look at your feet. Study them carefully. They are the most important equipment that you have. They are going to have to carry you on this journey. You might as well start right now with getting to know your feet.

Your feet are some genetic concoction that ended up at the bottom of your legs. You might have your great-grandmother's toes and your father's instep, but your feet are as unique to you as your fingerprint.

We don't care how pretty your feet are. One of us (Jenny) has pedicures all the time. One of us (John) is lucky to remember to cut his toenails before they turn into daggers. It doesn't matter what kind of feet you have. You just need to get to know them.

This is not a treatise on feet; it's just a way to get you started so you can avoid making some of the more common mistakes. So if you're sitting there barefoot, you're ready to go.

The first thing you have to figure out is whether you have a normal, high, or low arch. You need to know this because when we get around to talking about training shoes, you'll see that there are running shoes designed specifically for normal, high, or low arches. The easiest way to figure out what you have is to take the "wet foot" test. It's simple, and you can do it in the privacy of your own home.

You'll need a shallow pan (or bathtub) with about one-quarter inch of water in it and some plain paper. A brown paper bag is best, but anything that won't absorb the water will work.

Step into the water and get the entire bottom of one foot wet, front to back. Then, while standing, place that foot on the paper and push your weight into the foot. Repeat with the other foot.

You should be looking at one of three things: If you have a normal arch, you will be looking at something that looks a lot like a foot! You'll see a clear heel, an outer edge that leads to your toes, and an inner edge that breaks cleanly just in front of your heel and picks up again at the ball of your foot.

If you have a high arch, or rigid foot, you will see your heel and then a gap between the heel and the ball of your foot. There will often be no connection at all between the heel and the ball.

If you have a low arch, you're probably staring at a giant foot-like blob where everything from the heel to the toes, on the inside and outside, is connected.

It doesn't matter what kind of foot you have. It only matters that you know.

If you're eager to know a little more, try the same thing while seated. Compared the weighted foot outline with the unweighted one. If there is a huge difference, you may have a high arch but soft bones. Again, you just need to know.

Take a quick look at your toes while you're at it. Is your foot longest at the big toe? Is it longest at the second toe? Does the ball of your foot seem wide compared to your heel? You're now armed and ready to head to your nearest running specialty store to buy your first pair of running shoes.

Okay, you've got your shoes, you are following the first week of your running program, and you've made the time to do it. The first step you take can be the most daunting one of all. You are comfortable with what is behind you, but you are not sure about what lies ahead. This is the moment of truth. You could go back inside and go on with your life, or you could opt for what's behind door number two and actually start your running career.

Your first run should be challenging yet comfortable and fun. You should hear yourself breathe, but you shouldn't be gasping for air. You should run at a pace where you can finish the workout without collapsing at the end. You should feel empowered but also challenged. It won't be easy, but it shouldn't be impossible. If running were simple, everyone would be doing it.

The first week is loaded with motivation and enthusiasm. You're doing something new. You have new clothes and shoes. The key to getting through the week is to stick to your running program and avoid going farther, faster, higher . . . It can be enticing to run beyond that mark you hit earlier in the week, but please keep in mind that the impact of running is cumulative, and doing more sooner can hurt you in the coming weeks. Follow the plan, and you will adapt so quickly that you will be amazed at your transformation.

John's first run brought him to about 300 steps in front of his home—a quarter mile. A quarter mile is the distance he could run, walk, and waddle when he started. But that short distance gave him enough confidence and enthusiasm to make a mark 1.5 miles from his front door. It took him 6 months to reach that mark, but he did it. Rome wasn't built in a day, and our bodies adapt in their own time too.

Jenny's first official run with her friends was about 30 minutes in duration and about 2 miles in total—nothing that broke world records, but she sure was happy to finish with a smile on her face. She still remembers that first run because it was the first time she had gone farther than the end of her block without failing. In fact, she talked the whole way and was surprised when the run was done!

We made it through our first week, and so can you. Intensity is the key to moving on to week 2. The harder you push, the less you like it, the more you want to retire and hang up your shoes. We see this a lot with type A people like Jenny. The first workout, they are up at the front of the pack, wanting to go farther, faster, and they end up finishing last behind all the folks who are laughing and smiling as they cross the finish line of the training run.

Running on a treadmill for the first few workouts is one way to control your pace. It will give you an initial sense of what different paces feel like. Although treadmill running is slightly easier than running outdoors, it's a great way to get started. Treadmills are a little more forgiving with impact, and if you live in the mountains or rolling hills, you can start on flat terrain and build up to tackling the hills.

Another way to monitor pace and effort level is to go by how you feel. No, not a sad or happy feeling—more like easy, hard, or impossible. We use the i-Rate Scale to rate your effort level while running. It is a simple 1-to-10 scale, with 1 being easy or at rest (watching the latest reality show) and 10 being an all-out effort (wanting to throw up on your shoes).

For most runs, you should initially be at 6 to 7 on the scale, or at a "conversational pace." Conversational pace is—you guessed it—a running pace at which you can still talk. After all, this is supposed to be fun, right? We've solved some of the world's greatest problems on runs. So talking is key. If you barely get out "yes" and "no," you are running too hard. If you are gasping for air like you are climbing Mount Everest, you are running too hard. If you want to sock the person next to you for being happy and not struggling at all, you are running too hard.

The opposite of this is also true. You want to be able to have a conversation but not sing a song. So if you break out into a rendition of "The hills are alive with the sound of music," we will all know you aren't working hard enough.

If you want to go high-tech, you can use a heart rate monitor for instant feedback while running and walking. It is a very accurate means of monitoring your pace and effort. You can learn all about monitors and the significance of effort-based training in Chapter 16. For now, let's stick to the basics. Whether you go by the i-Rate Scale or heart rate, monitoring your effort is key for progressing to the next level and running wisely. You couldn't learn geometry without first learning your numbers and shapes in kindergarten, and you shouldn't run hard your first week or month.

This process should be challenging but not so hard that you hate it. Selecting the right program level based on your fitness and experience level, training at the right intensity and pace, and sticking to the program will launch you to the next week of training with a smile on your face and a pocket full of confidence.

## COACH JENNY'S TIPS AND TRICKS

✓ Always start your running career with a new pair of fitted running shoes. They will support you mile after mile and decrease your risk of injuries. Donate those old shoes that have grass stains. They won't make the cut in your running career.

✓ As long as you are shopping for shoes, toss in some technical socks too. They will prevent blisters from forming (see Chapter 16).

✓ Review your training program and get familiar with its structure. It was designed to prepare you for running a race, losing weight, or getting back into running regularly. Whatever your running goal, you may need to modify the program to fit it into your lifestyle.

✓ Begin each workout with a 5-minute walking warmup to gradually increase respiration and heart rate and prepare your body for the run. Finish every workout with an easy-paced walk to return gradually to a resting state.

✓ Put your workouts for the week in your planner or PDA. Once a workout is scheduled, it's harder to skip.

✓ Make it a priority. Put your scheduled "you" time before work, errands, or even relaxing.

✓ Schedule your workouts at the time of day that works best for you. If you are not a natural morning person, running first thing won't work for you.

✓ Run at a place that is convenient for you. Treadmill, trail, or road, if it isn't convenient, it's harder to squeeze into your schedule.

✓ Put a copy of your running program on the fridge or keep it with you at work, and remind yourself of your goal workouts for the week.

✓ Stick to the scheduled workouts and avoid adding more time or intensity, which can hurt you in the long run.

✓ Monitor your intensity wisely. If you run too fast or too hard, it becomes less fun, and the motivation to run again quickly diminishes. "No pain, no gain" is out, replaced by "Less is more."

# 10

# YOUR FIRST MONTH

I don't know if it's because I'm a man or not, but I was only ever really able to make any kind of change in my life or maintain any kind of enthusiasm for anything new for about 3 weeks. Three weeks! That's it. Of course, I'm also the guy with the television remote who's trying to watch two shows at the same time and the guy who can set his car radio to "search" and let it keep going around the dial, looking for a better song.

Over the course of my life, I wanted to be a lot of things. I just wanted to be them for only about 3 weeks. I wanted to be better at tennis, better at fishing, better at speaking Spanish. For about 3 weeks.

I wanted to lose weight, get in shape, learn to run, ride a bicycle, and on and on—for about 3 weeks.

The problem for many of us is that our enthusiasm for almost anything wanes after about 3 weeks. It doesn't seem to matter how fired up we are at the beginning or how committed we are or how dedicated we tell ourselves we're going to be; in about 3 weeks, we're discouraged and ready to quit.

It doesn't have to be that way.

I'm often asked why, at 43 and as out of shape as I was, I kept going. Why didn't I do what I had done so many times before? Why didn't I just quit after 3 weeks? You'll be surprised by my answer: I don't know.

It wasn't that it was any easier this time around than any other time. It wasn't that I suddenly discovered some untapped talent. It wasn't even that I was having all that much fun being active. But I think that, on some level, I was afraid that if I stopped *this* time, I'd never have the courage to try to get in shape again.

And on some other level I was angry—angry mostly at myself. Angry that I had allowed myself to believe that "fat is where it's at," that smoking makes you look cool, and that drinking and eating to excess were somehow a privilege that came with my age.

But I was also angry at the people in my life who reinforced all those misperceptions. I was angry at my drinking buddies, angry at those who passed me the extra food, and angry at a culture that lied to me about what I was doing to myself.

I took that anger and put it to work. Make no mistake: When it came to running, I stunk. Not just a little. It wasn't as if I was merely mediocre. I seriously stunk. So much so that I hid the fact that I was running from nearly everyone in my life. I even tried to hide it from the people I didn't know. When I'd run down the street, I'd try to hide from cars. If someone passed, I'd pretend that I was walking "somewhere," not walking just "anywhere."

What we see, though, in our training groups, clinics, and e-mails is that what makes people stop is not their lack of ability, but their expectations. And too often it's not even their own expectations. It's a set of expectations that they've borrowed from someone else or that someone else has given them.

It's the "brother-in-law syndrome." It seems like every new runner has a brother-in-law who is a runner or, worse, used to be a runner. This guy is almost always a leftover wannabe subelite who knows everything there is to know about running—or, rather, everything that was known about running 20 years ago.

If you've got a brother-in-law (or a friend or parent or spouse) like that, the first thing you need to do is politely tell him that while you appreciate his words of wisdom, this is something that you're going to figure out on your own. If he doesn't listen at first, be patient. He will.

You will only succeed if you are setting realistic expectations for yourself based on the uniqueness of who you've been, who you are, and who you want to be. You cannot and should not try to be what someone else is or was or wants you to be. You can't.

The only person who can truly judge and evaluate how you're doing is *you*. Your progress—fast or slow—is *your* progress. Your pace—fast or slow—is *your* pace. It's yours and yours alone. No one can take it from you.

As a columnist for *Runner's World* magazine since 1996, I've written well over 100 columns. One that continues to be among the most popular is titled "Working the Shovel," about my experience working as a laborer for the Norfolk and Western Railroad. Briefly: We were moving a big pile of rocks from where it was to where the foreman wanted it to be. Moving rock a shovelful at a time is back-breaking work. And that shovel will wear you out in a hurry.

The foreman was yelling, and I was doing everything I could to meet his expectations, but it was killing me. Then one of the veterans on the crew came up to me and said the words that changed my life that day and every day since. He said, "Son, ain't no man gonna break your back long as you workin' the shovel."

Simple. Eloquent. Brilliant. It wasn't the foreman that was making me work that hard. It was my fear of what the foreman would think or do or say.

In this first month of running, be aware of the tendency to live up to someone else's expectations. Find the training program that's right for you, and stick with it. Don't let yourself quit just because you don't think you're good enough.

I've coached thousands of runners through their first month of running. Although we are all different in many ways, in most cases, we learn to run the same way. Those first few weeks are chalked with patience and humility.

Practicing patience is key because running doesn't happen overnight. It develops one run at a time. Humility comes from being an adult and learning a new trick. Avoid comparing yourself to someone you know or the person next to you. Understand that some begin with walking, some with running and walking, but we all end up as runners somewhere along the way.

The first month of your running career is all about creating the habit. Figure out the best way to squeeze the runs into your busy lifestyle. It takes 21 days to create a new habit. Stick with it for 3 weeks straight, and I promise it will become second nature and, more important, a part of your lifestyle. When you cross into that fourth week, you know you're well on your way. Anyone can do anything for 3 weeks. Take it through 4 weeks, and you have yourself a new habit.

When setting up a spiral of dominoes on the floor, the key is to space them close enough to each other so when one falls, it hits another, and so on, creating a chain reaction. Running works the same way. Your running workouts need to be spaced close enough so you create muscle memory and avoid having to relearn how to run each week. First timers should start with every other day; this ensures proper recovery between workouts but is still often enough to create that running memory or chain reaction. Creating a running lifestyle happens over time. It won't feel easy the first time or even the 15th. Eventually, your body will adapt and become a runner and actually feel weird when you don't run.

## REST AND RECOVERY

You may have noticed that rest is a component of your training schedules. There are two types of rest: active and passive. Active rest is cross-training: cycling, swimming, strength, yoga—low-impact activities that rest the running muscles. Passive rest is just that: passive. It doesn't necessarily mean stretched out on the sofa, but it does mean little to no activity. Rest days are key because they allow your body to recover and rejuvenate from the running and cross-training days. Your body grows strong at rest.

Sometimes aches and pains creep into the picture. These are red flags; they're your body's way of communicating that something is wrong. Make sure you are wearing running shoes that fit properly. Running in shoes that are old, not made for running, or just don't fit well can and will create aches and pains and eventually injuries.

Developing pain in your first month of training can also be due to doing too much too soon. Running too hard is a big factor. Slow down and make sure you are running at a conversational pace. Running too far can also create problems, so begin with a conservative program and build slowly.

## BREATHING

Learning how to breathe is vital. It may sound funny, but the top question I receive on the trail is "Coach Jenny, how do I breathe when I run?" Although day-to-day breathing is automatic, it can get complicated when you run, as your body requires a higher volume of oxygen to move the working muscles. The faster you run, the more oxygen you need. If you find yourself struggling to breathe, gasping for air, or even getting side stitches, slow down. The number one error most runners make in their first month of running is going out too fast. It won't work, and you will end up hating the experience.

Once you've slowed down, breathing becomes like dancing. Try to match your breathing to your stride, or every time your foot hits the ground. Your breathing then becomes rhythmical and on tempo and is much more efficient. On an easy-paced run, you might breathe in for three or four steps and out three or four steps. If you are running faster, the tempo increases and becomes one-two, one-two, one-two. Try this test on your next run. You should be breathing at a tempo of three or four strides. If you are breathing faster, you are running too fast. Slow down and get on the right tempo. Your runs will be more enjoyable and your body will progress faster.

Breathe in and out through your mouth. Running is demanding and requires a lot of oxygen to get to the muscles. The easiest way to get the air in is through the largest hole. Trying to breathe through your nose is like breathing through a straw.

You may find that after the few first months, you fall off the band-wagon, so to speak. If you miss a few run workouts, go back a week or two in the training program and build back up again. If you miss more than 3 weeks, start from the beginning. If you stick with it, you will succeed. It took me four times to get it right. Don't look back and worry about what you didn't do; keep your focus forward on what you can do.

Never underestimate the power of a group. I learned with a group what I couldn't as a young girl trying to run down my block. The accountability, the support, and the social aspects work in unison to build a runner. I see it every season, when I coach new runners and walkers in our Learn to Run programs in my company, Chicago Endurance Sports. I built that company with my friend Mike Norman out of a passion for teaching people that it can be done and personal experience of not knowing how to do it on my own. Join a local group. You can find one at your local running stores and races. You will meet friends for life and people who share your joy in running.

Tracking your progress in a log is a great way to motivate your-self. It may not seem like much initially, but believe me, when you hit week 4 and begin to see changes and are able to go farther, it is great to look back at how far you've come. There are online logs and logbooks you can use. Note your run distance, time, temperature, shoes, and mood. A record is also helpful if you begin to have aches and pains; you can review your runs and see where you may have pushed too far or too fast—or maybe you need to replace your shoes. Your history becomes your motivation for the future.

You will know you are becoming a runner when you start saying things like "I 'only' have to run 30 minutes today" or when you drive the course you just ran to see how far you went. You'll know your body is adapting when the runs seem easier or when you run a little farther. Mostly, you will know you are becoming a runner when you get crabby when you *can't* run.

Your first month of running will be full of challenges. But like any new activity, week by week, your body will adapt and your mind will make friends with your inner runner. Remember, the first 30 days is all about creating a new habit. Be patient. Follow the training program. Look for the signs.

## COACH JENNY'S TIPS AND TRICKS

✓ Run like a Penguin. Running rewards the patient and reprimands the overzealous.

✓ Volunteer for a local race. You will quickly see the various shapes, sizes, and speeds on the course. Most of us are just out there to have fun and get a T-shirt. Plus, this will be good intel if you decide to run a race!

✓ Avoid adding running too hard or too often in the first month. The risk for injury will skyrocket, and the fun factor will drop. The training programs are developed to progress gradually to allow your body to adapt and get stronger.

✓ Listen to your body. Aches and pains are your body's way of alerting you that something is wrong. Take a few days off to heal; in most cases, the pain will disappear.

✓ Take the "talk" test. You should be able to speak without gasping or feeling out of breath. If you can't, then slow down.

✓ You should feel challenged when you run but "good" at the finish, like you could go a few more minutes.

✓ Practice patience. Patience and tenacity are key tools to have in your toolbox in the first month of running. Rome wasn't built in a day, and you won't become a runner overnight. Develop the tenacity to stick with it week to week.

✓ Don't compare yourself to anyone else. There will always be runners who are faster and can run farther. The only runner who is important is you.

✓ If you get a side stitch, focus on exhaling as the foot on the opposite side of the stitch hits the ground. So if you have a stitch on your right side, exhale as your left foot hits the ground. Slow your pace, and the stitch will disappear.

# 11

# YOUR FIRST YEAR

## JOHN'S FIRST YEAR

For nearly all new athletes, the first year is an exciting time. If you
started really out of shape, like I did, it just seems like the progress
is never going to end.

The first time I tried to run-walk a mile, it took me nearly 30
minutes. So you can imagine how good it felt when I got that down
to 25 minutes, and then 20, 15, 12, and so on. In fact, the very first
time I ran a mile in under 10 minutes, I went out and bought a pair

of racing flats like the elite runners wear. I figured I had done all I could do; the rest would come from better equipment.

Of course, that didn't work. I had fast shoes but slow feet. Truth is, I looked really cool and really fast right up to the point where they said *Go!* Then it was the same old slow guy in fancy new running shoes.

I also thought in that first year that I was going to somehow get to the point where I could be competitive in my age group. I was 44 years old or so. I was only competing against other 40- to 44-year-olds, who I figured started out in as bad a shape as I had, so I was sure to catch them.

I didn't.

But it wasn't from lack of trying. No sir. I read everything I could get my hands on about getting faster. I was doing intervals at the track. I was doing fartleks on the streets. I was doing everything imaginable to get faster. And I did. A little.

During my first year of running, I went from being truly terrible to merely mediocre. Actually, *mediocre* is probably an overstatement. There were times in some races when I approached mediocrity, but I couldn't do it on a regular basis.

We hear from people all the time who say that they are having a hard time staying motivated. It's a real problem, especially if you had dreams of getting to a point in your running that you realize now you are never going to get to.

What do you do?

I made a list of things that I couldn't do or hadn't done but wanted to do. Mostly it was races and distances and events that somehow piqued my curiosity. I wasn't sure how I was going to do those things, but I was certainly going to try.

I'd never run a 10-K, so that was the first major goal; 6.2 miles is a long way to go if you've never done it before. It's a long way to go even if you *have* done it before. But I knew that 10-K was a reasonable distance, so I set out to run one.

I didn't know what I was doing, but I figured I had to at least start increasing the distance of my runs. So, instead of going out for my normal 3-mile run, I just doubled it and started running 6 miles every time I ran.

It took about a week for that plan to fall apart.

Then I figured that maybe if I just stretched one run per week to 6 miles, that would do the trick. And it did. It wasn't long before I signed up for and completed my first 10-K. So far, so good.

For reasons that are still unclear to me today, I decided that my next goal should be to run a marathon. Again, I didn't know what I was doing, but at least I knew I couldn't run 26 miles every time I ran.

What I did figure out was that marathoners had to learn to run when their legs were tired. And because I couldn't run for more than 3 hours, I decided to do the next best thing: I would bicycle to exhaustion before I started to do my long runs.

After about a month of limping around, I took a week off and lined up at the marathon starting line. I ran to almost exactly mile 1 before my knee went out. I hobbled along with the motorcycle cop until mile six and then dropped out.

But believe it or not, I wasn't discouraged. Although it was true that I had failed, I had failed in such a monumental fashion at something so totally outrageous that somehow it didn't matter.

Then I decided I should try a triathlon, so I bought a Speedo bathing suit and headed for the swimming pool. I won't bore you with the details, but suffice it to say that a guy who loses 80 pounds should never, ever put on a Speedo, but if he does anyway, he should never go into a public area.

But somehow I managed to get through that first triathlon. Not well, though. In fact, I was dead last, but again, it didn't matter. I was doing it. And for me, doing it was more important than doing it well.

Then came the dream of a lifetime. I was going to attempt a half Ironman triathlon: a 1.2-mile swim, 56-mile bike ride, and 13.1-mile run. I did not have the faintest idea what I was doing, but I managed to do the training, get to the starting line, and finish. It was ugly, but I finished.

It was riding home after that event that I wrote what became the first "Penguin Chronicle" and appeared in *Runner's World* in May 1996. And it was in that column, written in the backseat of a minivan somewhere on an interstate highway in Georgia, that the words that have become a mantra for a generation of runners came out of my hands. In reflecting about that half Ironman, I wrote:

*The miracle isn't that I finished.*
*The miracle is that I had the courage to start.*

That thought has motivated me ever since. I am motivated not so much by what I can do and have done but by what I'm not sure I can do and haven't done. In the years since, this has given me a reason to take on every challenge that I can imagine.

What motivates you may be different, but whatever it is, you'll find it if you keep looking. And you may find out that running is just the beginning of a whole new life.

## JENNY'S FIRST YEAR

I knew how to run when I was a young girl. We all do. But when I tried again as an adult, I was chubby and running way too fast. I just couldn't figure out how to do what had seemed so easy in my youth.

My strategy of running as hard as I could to the end of the block wasn't working. I almost always ended up in tears and wouldn't try again for months.

The key to my success was finding a group to run with—a social connection. It was a way to learn from others and, more important, a way to find a pace that wouldn't make me feel like I was going into cardiac arrest. My first year of running was fun, challenging, exciting, and mysterious. I ran my first race, a 5-K in Milwaukee, and was beaten by a 72-year-old man at the finish. If that wasn't bad enough, they announced it on the PA system!

It didn't matter because when I crossed that finish line, I began to call myself a real runner. You too will call yourself a real runner. It may be on your first training run. It may be 6 months into your training. It may not be until you cross the finish in your first race. It doesn't matter. At some point in your first year, you will make that transformation and become a runner.

You will see the greatest improvements in your first year of running, especially if you are like I was—not even able to run down the block. Your heart will grow stronger and be able to pump more blood per beat, so your resting heart rate will most likely drop. Your muscles, tendons, and joints will all get stronger and be able to withstand the impact of running. You will run farther and faster and see more things on your route (unless you are on a treadmill).

Your runs will get easier. You will find yourself saying things like "I am only running 3 miles today" and "I *have* to get out for a run." You will definitely bore your family and friends to tears talking about your running. This first year, running will become a part of who you are.

You may find that your motivation declines with time, so set a specific goal. Run 3 miles in 30 minutes, participate in your first race, or run farther. Having an attainable goal will keep your motivation high and your runs consistent. There is nothing more motivating than having the accountability of a group of runners waiting for you. If you miss a run, they *will* ask where you were. Find a running buddy. Share stories and cover the miles with a friend. I call these "therapy runs." My girlfriend and I cover everything from world peace to family in a matter of miles. We never run out of things to talk about. That gets me up and out of bed in the morning.

You may miss a few runs here and there. Sometimes life gets in the way. Sickness, work, and family can all wreak havoc on your running life. If this happens, plan A is to shorten the run and get in what you can. We call this the Better than Nothing Run. It is better to run 25 minutes than not at all.

If you get sick, take the time you need to heal and recover. In most cases, it's safe to run if the illness is above your neck. If it goes down into your chest, rest. It's not worth the risk of making it worse. Taking 10 or more days off running is not fun, but it doesn't mean you have to start all over again. Start back with a 20- to 30-minute easy run. If that goes well, run three or four 30-minute easy-paced runs, then gradually build back to where you were. It typically takes your body double the amount of time you took off to return to where you were. If you miss 7 days, give yourself 2 weeks of easy running to build back up.

You will have run through several seasons this year. The trick to running in the heat is to allow your body 7 to 10 days to acclimate to warmer weather. It's amazing how our bodies adapt. I ran with an adventure-racing buddy in Death Valley in the middle of July. It was 130°F! We ran 135 miles across the desert and up a mountain. Although it may not be the healthiest endeavor, you can see that even in such extreme conditions, our bodies *do* adapt.

Your body will work extra hard to keep you cool during the first week until it adapts to the warmer temperatures. Run at cooler times of the day; wear sunscreen, sunglasses, and loose-fitting, light-colored clothing; and stay hydrated. If it's a heat-alert day, take your run indoors on a treadmill. If you do run outdoors, add power-walk breaks to bring your core temperature down. If you run-walk, add another minute to your walking portions. It works like a charm, and you'll sail through your workout in the hot weather. Once your body acclimates, you can resume regular training on most summer days.

Winter running is also tough, but it too can be done. In fact, it is my favorite running season. In most cases, it is cold but not freezing and blizzardy every day. Unless you are in northern Alaska or Antarctica, running outdoors in winter can be very pleasant. (Actually, I ran the Antarctica Marathon a few years ago, when the winds were 40 miles per hour and the windchill was well below zero. At times, there was 6 feet of snow to climb through. I made it successfully, but it was pretty tough. My legs never warmed up, even though I had plenty of layers on.)

For one thing, your body temperature increases when you run and adds about 15° to 20° to the outdoor temperature. Make sure you think about this when you dress for the run. A 35°F day feels like 50°F to a runner. Dress in layers with technical running apparel (as described in Chapter 16) so that if you overdress, you can shed something.

If the temps drop below 10°F, I typically take my runs inside. I get a better-quality workout and reduce the risk of injury from running on cold muscles. Avoid running on icy roads and paths. It is an easy way to get hurt. Snow-covered roads provide better traction. Shorten your stride and slow down when running on snow and ice. It's also helpful to wear Yaktrax or cleats. Like chains on car tires, they give you more traction on the snow. It's a good idea to run with a buddy when the going might be treacherous, and be sure to wear bright colors and reflective apparel on short, dark days.

Keep a log! It is a great resource for tracking the history of your running career—and you can watch your progress unfold right before your eyes. It is also useful to evaluate where you need to make improvements or took a wrong turn in training. Plus, it's fun to look back at how far you've come.

You will run through this first year just like life: through ups and downs. Some runs will feel easy and some not so easy. The hard days will humble you, and the easy days will bring you back for more. If you find yourself in the middle of a hard run that just feels like a slog, slow down. Your body is telling you it needs more time to sleep, defrag from work, or heal from an illness—or that it is just plain fatigued. It is better to take your workout down a couple of notches in intensity and complete an easy run than to soldier through and end up feeling worse than ever.

I have been running for more than 18 years now, and I still have runs that are tough. It is part of being a runner. All runners have hard and easy days. Just because the fast runners look so good doesn't mean they aren't struggling too. They are, just like you. It is a part of what makes running so rewarding. If it were easy, everyone would be doing it. The hard runs build character.

## COACH JENNY'S TIPS AND TRICKS

✓ Look for signs of improvement: going farther, getting faster, and calling yourself a runner.

✓ Set specific goals for your first year. It gives your training purpose and keeps you on track.

✓ When you achieve one goal, set another.

✓ Connect with a running club or find a running buddy. Accountability gets you going on the days you don't feel like running.

✓ Understand that running is challenging for everyone. But if you start with a conservative program and have patience, it will get easier.

✓ Be sure you stay hydrated. It's as important when running in the cold as in the heat.

✓ Look back at how far you've come this year. Celebrate your success.

# 12

# THE NEXT STEP

## JOHN'S NEXT STEPS

What do you do once you've done the impossible? What can you possibly do once you've done everything you ever imagined you could do? What do you do when you've exceeded your wildest dreams?

You do more.

Remember that first week of running? At that point, you probably couldn't imagine running 1 minute or 1 mile. You probably couldn't imagine that with patience and tenacity, you would become a real runner. And yet, here you are.

Now what?

For me, this was where the real fun began. Once I had satisfied all the old dreams, once I had slain all the old dragons and overcome all the old demons, I was free to become the runner and athlete that I wanted to be.

Once I was liberated from needing to prove something to myself or someone else, once I didn't always have to run farther or faster, I could find much better reasons to run. After I had done everything I thought I could do, I was ready to do everything else.

Almost overnight, everything about my running got better. I enjoyed it more, did it more, and looked forward to it more. I discovered that I could be a runner even when I wasn't running. I learned how to be an athlete—how to think, feel, and live like an athlete. And I didn't have to beat myself up to do it.

I discovered that I was choosing races that I wanted to run because I wanted to run them. I found myself going back to races I had run before so I could run them again with a new attitude. I found myself searching out people and places to run that I thought would just be fun to do.

I also found myself willing to take on new challenges with less fear. Not *without* fear, mind you. But with *less* fear. I was no longer paralyzed by my fear, even if I didn't run blindly into every new experience.

What you do as your next step is completely up to you. But I can tell you a few of the things that I tried. You might like to try them too.

**Hiking:** Okay, this might not sound like a very big deal to you, but for a former smoker, drinker, and overeater, the idea of heading off on a daylong hike with nothing but what I could carry on my back was pretty intimidating. In the old days, I never would have done it because I wouldn't have been able to carry all the beer I needed.

I found myself hiking along the Na Pali Coast in Hawaii. I was wearing funny-looking rubber shoes, carrying an honest-to-goodness adventure-racing backpack, and climbing around on rocks and roots and getting wet and laughing my head off. It was like being a kid all over again.

And I found myself hiking up Mount Baker outside of Bellingham, Washington. Before, anything starting with *Mount* would have been enough to get me to turn around and head home. But again, I had some funny-looking shoes, a backpack with a water bladder, and pants with zip-off legs. I also had a watch that told me the altitude, and I was having a ball. I was exploring the world the same way I explored my neighborhood as a young child.

**Snowshoeing:** This is a little bit like hiking, except that it's bitterly cold and you end up covered in snow. But there I was at Lake Louise in Banff, Canada, in the dead of winter with the high temperature of about 15°F above zero, snowshoeing up the Beehive overlook. Me—a guy who used to keep an engine warmer on my car so it wouldn't be cold when I started it up—snowshoeing in the cold, in the snow. Amazing.

**Kayaking and canoeing:** Paddling along in Resurrection Bay off of Seward, Alaska, I saw the first bald eagle I had ever seen not in captivity. I cried. The eagle was in the wild, and so was I. I was experiencing a moment so human that I was stunned.

I paddled a canoe backward through the rapids on the New River in Virginia. My paddling partner and I couldn't figure out how to keep the canoe going forward, so we went through every piece of white water backward. And I had a ball.

**Mountain biking:** When I was a kid, we used to ride our 40-pound Schwinn Springer bicycles along the Des Plaines River Path. We didn't know that it was a mountain-bike trail. It probably wasn't in those days. We just thought it was cool to go pedaling for all we were worth through the woods. I found the same joy pedaling along a ridge outside of Park City, Utah, and along an isolated desert path near Bingham, New Mexico, and in the beautiful scenery near Yellowstone Park.

But it doesn't have to be exotic. Just pounding around the trails near home is enough to put a huge smile on my face.

**Road biking:** This is really a carryover from where this whole period of my life began. I was too heavy at first to run, so I started with biking. As I discovered how much I liked running, the biking slowly faded away. But once I was free of my own limitations, I was back out there on the streets. Now at least some of the dreaming I do has to do with long bicycle rides.

**Adventure racing:** This was more a concession to my curiosity than anything else. Jenny is a world-class adventure racer. She's done the toughest races of all time, the Eco-Challenges. I wasn't thinking of anything like that. But I did do a 24-hour race and a 2-day race. I ran and hiked and navigated and paddled and basically had the best time of my life.

The secret to all of this? I'm not any good at any of it! I'm just having fun, and that's all that matters. And you can too.

## JENNY'S NEXT STEPS

My next steps were a little different from John's. He had competed at the top of his game in the music world and wanted his life of fitness to be all about the joy of the journey. I, on the other hand, wanted to run farther and faster and see just how far I could go. I had finally figured out how to run and, in the process, ignited my competitive side.

My first year of running was one of the best times of my life. I learned how to run regularly and go farther, faster, and I even lost a little weight. I trained to run a 5-K, 10-K, half marathon, and marathon. More important, I developed a self-confidence that was never there before.

Running changed my life. I felt good about myself. I developed new, healthy friends. I traveled to races and ran through cities. I chiseled away at my race times and the fears that kept my dreams dormant. I felt like a kid again, running, skipping, and catching frogs. I woke the adventurer in me. I wanted to see just how far I could go.

The ultimate standard for a runner is the Boston Marathon. You have to qualify to even get in. It is based on age and gender, and it's a pretty tough challenge. There I was, someone who never thought she could run down the block, now thinking about Boston. Could I do it? The mere challenge of the impossible was what motivated me. That is also what fueled the next year of my life. It took me two marathons and many months of training, but I successfully qualified for and ran the Boston Marathon. Even today, I can hardly believe it.

I've had some great conversations during runs with my buddies on the trails. It was the one with Shelly that propelled me into the most adventurous ride of my life.

Shelly mentioned that she was doing an adventure race with two of her male friends. I had never heard of adventure racing but was intrigued. She explained that you have to race together; you navigate with a compass and map and mountain bike, kayak, run, and hike, and you get really dirty. Oh, and it starts at midnight! She had me at *compass*, *dirt*, and *midnight*. This sounded like the perfect sport for a girl who grew up playing with frogs and exploring the quarry behind her house. Sign me up!

My first adventure race was called the Pathfinder Challenge. It was in southwestern Wisconsin and lasted about 8 hours. We started on a lake at midnight, kayaking in inflatable boats during a thunderstorm. I was hooked on the sport by the time we reached land. The team had hoped to finish strong but ended up winning the darn thing, and that was it. The next 7 years of my life became all about running and adventure racing.

At the time, adventure racing wasn't very popular. There were only a handful of races in the world: the Pathfinder Challenge, a few short races in California, and the Eco-Challenge. I think you know what is coming next: Hey, we just won an 8-hour race! We should put our name in the lottery to race the Eco-Challenge!

The Eco is billed as the World's Toughest Endurance Race. Eighty coed teams from all over the world race 24 hours a day, over a rugged 300-plus-mile course, trekking, running, whitewater canoeing, horseback riding, sea kayaking, mountain biking, scuba diving, and mountaineering.

We got into the lottery for Eco-Challenge Borneo, a jungle race in Malyasia, halfway around the world. The next 16 months of my life I ate, slept, and breathed Eco-Challenge.

There is no guarantee of finishing an Eco-Challenge. In fact, it is common for 80 percent of the teams to drop out in the first half of the race. Although we spent the better part of a year and a half training and preparing, Team Synterra had to drop out 8 days into the race. One teammate got sick, and the other was suffering from a waterborne bacterial infection.

Not long after I returned from Borneo, I received a call from a California team that was racing the next one in New Zealand. They needed an experienced female, and I was on the list. I was raring to go. I had unfinished business with the Eco-Challenge.

I trained and prepared and packed again. After more than 7 days of nonstop racing, Team Block reached the finish line.

I went on to race another Eco-Challenge in Fiji, and I raced solo events and orienteering events. I raced until I had accomplished every goal I set for myself.

Adventure racing gave me a life's worth of lessons—a doctorate in life. I found my strengths, revealed my weaknesses, and faced my fears. I learned to trust and trusted enough to learn. The journey revealed the essence of who I am and what I can do in my life, a gift I will always be grateful for.

This is why I don't laugh when people ask me, "Can I really do this? Can I run? Can I run a race? Can I complete a marathon?" I know you can. If a girl who once couldn't run down the block without crying can, you can too.

Running can be the foundation for your next adventure. When you are fit, you can explore the world. You can see, touch, hear, and smell the mountains. You can go farther or higher or faster. It all starts with having the courage to take that very first step and the patience and tenacity to stick with it. Set a goal for yourself, and see just how far you can go.

## COACH JENNY'S TIPS AND TRICKS

✓ Never say never. You never know what is around the next corner.

✓ Set a goal just beyond your reach. Challenge yourself to go beyond your perceived limits.

✓ Experiment with your fitness. Try a new activity. It will spice up your running regimen, use different muscles, and maybe even teach you something new!

✓ Don't fear failure. Some of the greatest lessons learned have been from mistakes. Failing is not the end; it is the start of learning how to improve.

# SECTION IV
## BECOMING A BETTER RUNNER

# 13

# FLEXIBILITY AND INJURY PREVENTION

Running in its essence is one of the most primal human movements. Sure it's demanding, but it is a natural movement. You can run almost anywhere, anytime. You don't need a lot of equipment. It's simple. We were built to run.

But like most things in life, if you do too much too soon or overdo it, your risk for aches and pains, and eventually injuries, rises. Some people can run like Forrest Gump, all the time and every day. Most mortals need rest days, cross-training, strengthening exercises, and flexibility training to run successfully. A well-rounded running program will almost always ensure a low risk for injury.

Many things can contribute to aches and pains and injuries. The hamstrings; hip flexors; iliotibial bands; piriformis; and calf, chest, and neck muscles are vulnerable to becoming inflexible and tight, making a runner vulnerable to developing injuries. Strength imbalances in opposing muscles, improperly fitting shoes, unsafe running surfaces, and drastic increases in mileage or speed can all wreak havoc on your running career. The good news is that you are reading this chapter, so you will learn how to prevent injuries from keeping you off the running trail.

Think of a hinge on a door. It has two anchor points and is attached to the door and the wall. When working efficiently, the door swings open and closes freely without obstruction. If, however, the hinge is too tight, the door will not open or close through the full range of motion, and you end up squeezing through the door every time you pass through it—never a good option. But if you force the door open, it may snap off the hinge.

Tight muscles work very much the same way. If your hamstrings are tight, your leg will not move through the full range of motion, and the length of your stride will be compromised. Moreover, you leave your muscles, joints, and tendons open to injury, much like the hinge. Flexible muscles are a key component in running injury free and to your greatest potential.

If you lifted a 10-pound dumbbell up and down for three days straight, the muscles in that arm would become very strong. However, all the other muscles in your body would remain untrained. Running strengthens some but not all muscles, which can leave your body unbalanced.

Muscular balance is important to allow opposing muscles to work together optimally. To extend your leg, the hamstrings in the back of your thigh must extend and lengthen while the quadriceps in the front of your thigh contract and shorten. If there is muscle tightness in the hamstrings and weakness in the quads, that motion becomes much more challenging, and the knee joint is compromised as well. It's important to strengthen and lengthen opposing muscles to decrease the risk for injury and increase the range of motion, stability, and strength of your muscles, joints, and tendons. We'll discuss strength training in the next chapter.

The surface you run on can also contribute to developing injuries. The uneven terrain of banked or cambered roads can cause knee and iliotibial band problems. Concrete sidewalks are tough on the body because the landing surface is very hard. When possible, avoid those two situations. Gravel or dirt paths are quite possibly the best running surfaces, as they are much more forgiving on the body and provide a softer, less shocking landing. As a rule of thumb, try to alternate your running on trails, roads, paths, and even treadmills. That way, your body adapts to a variety of terrains.

Finally, in my experience as a coach, the most common way runners get hurt is by increasing mileage or intensity too quickly and/or too drastically. Because running is a high-impact activity, progressions in training need to be very gradual. Each runner advances at his or her own rate, but a good rule is to progress no more than 10 percent each week. That way, your body is challenged but still recovers run to run and adapts to do more the next week.

Running injuries don't have to happen. Listen to your body as you progress, and make the appropriate modifications to your program if your body talks to you. There are several levels of pain, and you'll be happy to hear that not all pain requires you to stop running. Our friends and physical therapists from Athletico Sports Medicine in

Chicago have outlined the types of pain and just what you should do if it happens to you.

**Pain after running only:** If pain occurs only postrun and goes away quickly, consider taking a day or two off running and instead cross-train with an activity that does not aggravate the pain. Ice the area and focus on flexibility training. In most cases, this is enough to make the ache go away.

**Pain during and after running that does not affect your gait:** Take 3 or 4 days off running and ice, stretch, and cross-train. It is also recommended to schedule an appointment with a sports medicine doctor or physical therapist (PT) to evaluate and treat the pain, preferably someone who works with runners. Check with your local running store for references, as these shops typically partner with running-friendly professionals. I promise you they will get you back on the road, not tell you to stop running for the rest of your life.

**Constant pain that affects your gait:** If pain causes you to alter your running form and persists postrun, don't mess around—go get medical advice. Running through this type of pain will only make things worse and put you out of commission for a very long time. A PT or sports medicine specialist will evaluate the problem, figure out why it is happening, and then rehab the injury so it never happens again. In other words, he or she will get you running again!

Although it's important to understand the progression of pain, in most cases it can be prevented in the first place. One way you can decrease your risk of injury is to include the following flexibility exercises in your running routine.

The foam roller exercises for the iliotibial band and piriformis are lengthening exercises that work much like rolling out dough. You can also roll your calves, back, thighs (front and back), and even your shins. For a particular ache or tightness, use the foam roller in the morning and evening and prior to your runs.

The rest of the exercises are static, or holding, stretches specific to the needs of runners. The best time to perform these stretches is after running or cross-training, when the muscles are warm and pliable. Flexibility training can also promote faster healing workout to workout.

Why not stretch to warm up? Because the best warmup for running is running. The optimal warmup includes 3 to 5 minutes of brisk walking to raise your respiration, heart rate, and body temperature, followed by 3 to 5 minutes of easy-paced running.

If you are short on time and can't get to all the flexibility exercises, at least stretch the hamstrings, calf muscles, and hip flexors, and do the iliotibial band (ITB) foam roll. These areas tend to be the most vulnerable to tightness due to running.

## ITB Foam Roll

**Target Area:**

Iliotibial band (the long ligament running down the outside of the thigh)

**How-To:**

Although this move can be slightly painful, it is very effective in reducing knee pain due to ITB tightness. Lie on your side and position a foam roller under your hip. Put your top foot and both hands on the floor for stability.

Use your arms to slowly roll your body over the foam from just below the hip to just above the knee. Work your way back and repeat 10 times.

**Coach's Tip:**

*Make sure the side of your leg or ITB is on the foam. Keep the motion slow and controlled. If you get to a sensitive spot, hold and let the ITB relax into the foam. A progression is to roll with both legs straight and off the floor.*

## Piriformis Foam Roll

**Target Area:**

Sitting muscles (deep buttocks)

**How-To:**

The piriformis, located deep inside the buttocks, is a common place for tightness and pain. This exercise releases tightness, reduces pain, and improves hip mobility.

Sit on the foam roller and place one ankle on the opposite knee. Shift your weight onto the hip with the straight leg and roll slowly and gently over that hip.

## Coach's Tip:

*When you feel a tight spot, hold that position, relax the muscle, and place as much of your body weight on this spot as possible. You will feel your muscle release into the foam.*

# Downward-Facing Dog

## Target Areas:
Back of thigh, calf

## How-To:

Starting in a pushup position, press your body up and into an inverted V. Keeping your arms and legs straight, press your head through your arms, and keep your heels on the floor. Breathe and hold for 30 seconds. Repeat a second time.

**Coach's Tip:**

*This is a very effective yoga position and a great tool for runners as well because it elongates your hamstrings. Keep your feet straight and pointing toward your head.*

## Hip Flexor Lunge

**Target Area:**

Front of thigh

**How-To:**

Kneel on the floor with a mat under your knee, and put your right foot forward so the right knee is bent at 90 degrees and over the foot. Relax your left leg and focus on curling your left hip up toward the ceiling. Relax and hold for 20 to 30 seconds.

**Coach's Tip:**

*Keep your torso tall as you press your hip forward and up.*

## Hamstring Stretch

**Target Area:**
Back of thigh

**How-To:**

Stand with one leg elevated about 2 feet off the ground on a bench, stair, or chair. Keep the elevated leg straight, toes pointed toward the ceiling. Stand tall through the leg on the ground, hips facing forward. Lean gently forward from the hips while keeping the chest tall. Relax and hold for 20 to 30 seconds. Switch legs and repeat.

**Coach's Tip:**

*Focus on relaxing your upper body, hips, and legs while holding the stretch.*

## Calf Stretch

**Target Area:**
Lower calf

**How-To:**

Stand with your feet apart, one foot forward and one back, and bend the front knee gently. When you feel a stretch in the calf of the back leg, slowly and gradually bend that leg at the knee. Relax and hold for 20 to 30 seconds. Switch legs and repeat.

**Coach's Tip:**

*Make sure your feet are facing forward.*

## Inner Thigh Stretch

**Target Area:**

Inner thigh

**How-To:**

Sit with the soles of your shoes together. Hold your feet and gently press down on your legs with your elbows. Relax and hold for 20 to 30 seconds.

**Coach's Tip:**

*If this is too challenging, put your hands on the floor next to your knees and lean forward into the stretch.*

# Quad Stretch

**Target Area:**

Quadriceps (front of thigh)

**How-To:**

Stand with one foot on the floor and the other foot resting behind you on a bench or chair, just below hip height. Standing tall, focus on pushing your hips forward to feel the stretch up the thigh and in your hip flexors. Relax and hold for 20 to 30 seconds. Switch legs and repeat.

**Coach's Tip:**

*Keep your knees in alignment and hips facing forward.*

# Hip Stretch

**Target Area:**

Outer thigh

**How-To:**

Lie on your back with your right foot on the floor. Rest your left ankle just below your right knee and pull your right leg into your chest. Relax and hold for 20 to 30 seconds. Switch sides and repeat.

**Coach's Tip:**

*If this is too challenging, keep the right foot on the floor and sit up so your weight rests on your elbows or hands.*

## Gluteal Stretch

**Target Areas:**

Piriformis, gluteal muscles (buttocks)

**How-To:**

Lie on your back and cross your right leg over your left leg. Pull both legs into your chest to feel the stretch deep inside the gluteals. Relax and hold for 20 to 30 seconds. Repeat the stretch on both legs. Switch sides and repeat.

**Coach's Tip:**

*If it is too difficult to reach your knees, wrap a towel around your knees to use as leverage and pull the towel to your chest.*

## Chest Stretch

**Target Areas:**

Chest, shoulders

**How-To:**

Interlock your fingers behind your lower back. Keeping your arms straight, raise your hands up toward the ceiling until you feel a stretch in your chest and the front of your shoulders. Hold for 20 to 30 seconds and repeat.

**Coach's Tip:**

*You can also perform this stretch by holding on to a fence, pole, or anything behind you that is stable.*

## Back Stretch

**Target Areas:**
Upper and lower back

**How-To:**

Kneel on the floor and walk your hands out in front of your body. Shift your hips back, placing your weight on your heels while reaching forward with your hands. Hold for 20 to 30 seconds and repeat.

**Coach's Tip:**

*Relax your head between your arms. For an added bonus, walk your hands to the right side and hold, then repeat on the left side.*

world of running is much different today than it was 20 years ago. Strengthening your body will not only reduce injury risk but improve running performance. I promise.

Investing a little time in developing and maintaining a strong body will allow you to run healthily for the rest of your life. Sure, it takes away from the time you run, but the benefit of dedicating a few workouts each week to strength far outweighs foregoing it altogether to run more.

Most runners these days don't define themselves by just running. They also take yoga classes to improve flexibility, perform strength training to build a strong foundation, and alternate running with other activities like cycling and swimming to actively rest. The end result: They will run longer with better quality, and they may even have more fun!

Think of your body as a house. Would you like a house made of cardboard? It wouldn't withstand the first heavy rainfall that rolled through. How about building your house out of concrete and brick? Imagine a home so strong that even the worst storm can't affect it. That, my friends, is what strength training is to a runner.

Running is a high-impact activity. That doesn't mean it is bad for you; it just means that when you run, the impact on your body is higher than that of most activities. If you run without a strong foundation, it's like riding out a storm in a house made of cardboard. Before long, things will probably hurt, get out of balance, and stop you from running. That doesn't have to happen. Build a strong foundation by developing the right balance in your running muscles (that propel you forward) and the stabilizing muscles (that support you stride for stride).

This chapter is dedicated to showing you a few key strengthening exercises you can do two or three times a week to remodel your house with concrete and brick and, more important, allow you to run for a lifetime. These moves will benefit your running performance as well as decrease the risk of injury.

Put another way: Like the parts of a car, every element of running has a unique function. The engine and transmission are the forces that move the car, the fuel system helps the engine do its job, and the shocks and springs keep it stable while you drive down the street. Everything works together.

The primary force-producing muscles are like the engine of a car; they propel you from one foot to another. These muscles include the hamstrings (at the back of the thigh), hip flexors (at the top and front of the thigh), and the calves (two large muscles in the lower back leg). The assisting or secondary muscles in the thighs (quads), shins, and upper body help the primary muscles propel you forward.

The shocks and springs, or the stabilizing muscles in the core, adductors (inner thigh), and abductors (outer thigh), work to stabilize the joints, whether you're active or inactive. Without shocks and springs, your car would hop all over the road, side to side, up and down. Your body would do much the same without strong stabilizing muscles. Things that shouldn't move would and things that should move would not, leaving you open to injury and muscle imbalance. The stabilizing muscles have the toughest job, as they constantly work to keep your body stable while you forcefully run down the street.

The real secret to running strong and injury free is to maintain the balance between all three systems. If the stabilizing muscles are left untrained, the primary movers will take over and create an imbalance. To prevent a small coup from happening in your body, incorporate a well-rounded strengthening program that includes exercises for the primary movers, secondary movers, and stabilizing muscles.

There are hundreds of strength exercises you can do. The ones here are specific to the needs of runners and are some of my favorites. I like to call them *functional* because they are. There is no "riff-raff" or wasted energy. Every exercise has a purpose. If you give this program 8 to 10 weeks of consistency, you will begin to notice a difference in your running performance, speed, and daily activities. A little goes a long way. Give it a try.

Pay particular attention to the tips on form. It is better to perform an exercise with less weight or resistance with good form than to do it with more weight and terrible form. These are not traditional strength exercises. You won't find hack squats or 300-pound barbell bench presses. Runners don't need a lot of muscle in one place; they need balanced strength in a lot of places. What may look like an easy exercise is actually very difficult if done with good form (you may even see me sweating in the pictures).

You don't need a gym to perform these exercises, but you will need a few pieces of equipment or fitness toys: a fitness ball, resistance tube, resistance band (optional), foam roll, playground ball or towel, and a pair of light dumbbells (optional).

## FREQUENCY

If you are new to strength training, start by performing the following exercises twice per week on nonconsecutive days, maybe Monday and Thursday. You can do them after a short, easy run or after a 10-minute walking warmup. In either case, make sure you warm up prior to beginning this program.

If you are a seasoned strength-training person, include two or three strength sessions per week on nonconsecutive days (Monday-Wednesday-Friday or Monday-Thursday). Two sessions are plenty for runners during in-season training for a race (10K or half marathon).

Increase to three sessions in the off-season, when you aren't training as intensely. For those who race year-round (I know you are out there), stick with twice per week.

## INTENSITY

If you're just getting into strength training or returning after a long vacation from it, start with one set of 12 to 15 repetitions. Regardless of reps and sets, the key to getting the most out of the program is to take each exercise to fatigue—meaning, do the exercise until you can no longer perform the movement with good form. If you don't fatigue the muscle, you are wasting your time. That doesn't mean grunting to the point that everyone is looking at you, like something out of *Rocky*. It simply means focusing on each exercise and progressing as your body becomes stronger and fitter.

The biggest mistake most people make with strength is repeating the same exercises at the same intensity. It can always be more challenging. Just ask John. When he gets good at one exercise, I tweak it to make it tougher. Although he looks at me like I am Cinderella's evil stepmother, he gets stronger with each progression.

If you have been training with strength exercises, go with multiple sets of 8 to 12 repetitions. Because you have a baseline of strength, you can mix it up a bit. You can alternate a hard day (three sets of eight to 12 reps per exercise) with an easy day (one or two sets of 12 to 15 reps). Just like with running, there should be hard strength days and moderate days. You can even mix days of hard legs/easy upper body and core with days of hard upper body and core/easy legs. There is no one recipe that works. There's no magic pill. Make it fit your running program, your interests, and your lifestyle.

These exercises will get easy as your body adapts and grows stronger. Follow the tips to progress the exercise and make it more challenging. If you are just going through the motions, you won't continue to improve. Every exercise should be a challenge.

Initially, this program may take you 45 minutes. Once you learn the exercises, it is realistic to get through it all in 30 minutes. The strength routine is a great complement to cardio cross-training or a short run (but do cardio before strength training).

## NOTES ON BREATHING AND FORM

Because you use momentum when moving quickly, slow each exercise down to a controlled motion to increase the intensity of the contraction and minimize the risk of injury. Breathe in during the easier part of the exercise and out during the contraction, or hard part.

It is vital to maintain good posture and neutral alignment of your spine while performing these exercises. I like to say, "Maintain a strong core by drawing your navel toward your spine during each movement."

## HARD/LIGHT WORKOUTS

If you are new to strength training, include all the "light" exercises for the first 8 weeks. Then progress to include the "light + hard" exercises.

If you are already strength-training, use the light workout for one session and the hard for the other, especially if you are training for a long-distance race like a marathon. This will give you variety workout to workout and the flexibility to get your running and cross-training in too.

# WARMING UP

Spend 5 to 10 minutes warming up on a piece of cardio equipment, walking, or even running before you begin the strength program. It will raise your core body temperature, warm your muscles, and prepare you for the strenuous workout. Strength training can also be done after your cardio cross-training or run workouts.

## STANDING LUNGE [LIGHT + HARD DAYS]

**Target Muscles:**
Front and back of thigh, buttocks

**How-To:**

Stagger your feet front and back and about hip-width apart. Take an exaggerated step forward. Try to perform this one in front of a mirror so you can check your knee angle. Keeping your core in good alignment, bend the front knee 90 degrees, so the thigh is parallel with the floor. Make sure the knee is over the ankle and not beyond the toes (you should not feel this move in your knees). Pause and push through your front heel to return to the starting position.

**Progression:**

*Hold dumbbells and alternate from the starting position: Lunge forward with your right leg, then your left, and so on. To incorporate balance and stability work, put your front foot on a pillow or folded exercise mat.*

**Coach's Tip:**

*Focus on moving through the front leg in a downward motion toward the floor. You may feel this in the rear leg, as it is stabilizing, and the hip flexors are in a stretched position. You may also notice that you are stronger or more balanced on one side than the other. This is a challenging exercise as it trains each leg independently, which aids in balancing strength in both legs.*

## WALL SQUAT WITH BALL [LIGHT + HARD DAYS]

**Target Muscles:**
Front and back of thigh, buttocks, inner thigh

**How-To:**

Put a fitness ball between the middle of your back and a wall. Stand with your feet hip-width apart and take a few steps forward and away from the wall. Press your body firmly into the ball. Bend your knees to 90 degrees until your thighs are parallel to the floor and your knees are over your ankles (not your toes). Pause for a moment, then press through your heels and extend your legs to return to the starting position.

**Progression:**

*Hold dumbbells or a medicine ball. Even harder: Lift one foot and perform the exercise one leg at a time.*

**Coach's Tip:**

*Focus on pressing through each foot and leg evenly. Slowly bend and extend your legs, pausing briefly each time.*

## STEPUP [HARD DAY]

**Target Muscles:**

Front and back of thigh, buttocks

**How-To:**

Holding light dumbbells, stand facing a bench 18 to 24 inches high (a cooler, park bench, gym bench, or stable chair works well). Step up onto the bench with your right foot and push off with your left foot. While standing on the bench on your right foot, raise the left leg up to waist height and pause. Step down with your left foot. Perform the entire set on your right leg, then repeat with the left leg.

**Progression:**

*Don't put your foot back down to the floor to rest; lower it almost to the floor and then lift it back up. Even harder: Add a hop at the top of the bench.*

**Coach's Tip:**

*Keep your torso tall, and avoid leaning to one side. If this is too challenging, drop the weights and lower the bench height. Step with your entire foot on the bench and push through the heel. This is a great exercise for developing balance.*

# LATERAL LUNGE [HARD DAY]

**Target Muscles:**

Front and back of thigh, buttocks, inner thigh

**How-To:**

Stand tall with your feet hip-width apart. Step to the right, and with your weight on your right leg, squat by moving your hips back and down toward the floor. Keep your left leg straight and your toes facing straight ahead. Pause and return to the starting position. Repeat on the other side.

**Progression:**

*Hold a light (2- to 3-pound) medicine ball or dumbbell, and raise it to shoulder level while you step and squat. Even harder: Repeat the entire set of lateral lunges on one leg, and then switch to the other leg.*

**Coach's Tip:**

*Focus on moving through the lead leg while keeping the following leg straight. This works to lengthen as well as strengthen the inner thigh and groin area. Be cautious; avoid stepping too far out the first few times, and gradually progress to the side-step distance.*

# HAMSTRING CURL ON BALL [HARD DAY]

**Target Muscles:**

Back of thigh, buttocks, core

**How-To:**

Lie on your back with your hands by your sides on the floor, calves resting on a fitness ball, feet flexed with toes pointing toward the ceiling. Using your gluteal muscles (buttocks), squeeze and lift your hips off the floor until you make a diagonal line from your feet to your shoulders. Push down on the ball with your heels, and pull the ball toward your buttocks. Keep your hips and buttocks lifted while moving. Slowly straighten your legs as you push the ball away from you. When your legs are straight, lower your buttocks to the floor and repeat.

**Progression:**

*Keep your buttocks off the floor during each repetition. Even harder: Put your hands on your stomach and elbows on the floor while you perform the exercise, or try the exercise using one leg while keeping the unused leg bent and elevated.*

**Coach's Tip:**

*This is a great exercise to develop strength, balance, and stability. Focus on keeping your toes pointed toward the ceiling during the entire exercise. Press down and into the ball as you bend and extend your legs.*

## BRIDGE WITH BALL [LIGHT + HARD DAY]

**Target Muscles:**

Buttocks

**How-To:**

Lie on your back on the floor with your hands by your sides and a playground ball, rolled-up towel, or foam roller between your knees.

Using your gluteal muscles (buttocks), squeeze and lift your hips off the floor until you form a diagonal line from your knees to your hips and shoulders. Only your shoulders and feet remain on the floor. While lifting, press your knees into the ball and contract your buttocks muscles, squeezing in an up-and-in motion. This will activate the gluteal and adductor (inner thigh) muscle groups. Pause for a few seconds while holding the squeeze, then lower your hips back to the floor, continuing to press into the ball, and repeat.

**Progression:**

*Lower to a few inches off the floor instead of all the way down between reps. Even harder: Place your arms on your stomach, or try the exercise with one leg (without the ball).*

**Coach's Tip:**

*Draw your navel into your spine, and focus on two motions: pressing into the ball or towel and squeezing up toward the ceiling.*

## SIDE-LYING LEG RAISE [LIGHT + HARD DAY]

**Target Muscles:**

Hips (Abductors)

**How-To:**

Place a resistance band around your ankles (or perform this exercise without a band). Lie on your side with your head relaxed on your arm and one leg on top of the other. Keeping your legs straight, lift the top leg (with the foot flexed) to just above hip level, focusing on contracting your hip. Pause for one count, lower, and repeat.

**Progression:**

*Pause the extended leg at the top position during each repetition. Even harder: Use a band with a more challenging resistance level.*

**Coach's Tip:**

*Keeping your body in a long line on the floor, gently lean the top hip toward the floor. This isolates the abductors (hips) and keeps the thigh (quads) from performing all the work.*

## CALF RAISE [LIGHT + HARD DAY]

**Target Muscles:**

Calves

**How-To:**

From a pushup position, press up and put your right foot over your left heel. With your body weight on the ball of your left foot, press and raise your left heel off the ground. Hold for a few seconds, then push your left heel down toward the ground. Repeat.

**Progression:**

*Move your leg farther away to the side of your body.*

**Coach's Tip:**

*Focus on pressing the moving heel into the ground after each repetition for a great calf stretch.*

## HEEL WALK [LIGHT + HARD DAY]

**Target Muscles:**
Shins

**How-To:**

In a standing position, rock back on your heels and walk forward for 1 minute. Take a break and repeat. Perform only 2 reps.

**Progression:**

*Increase to 90 seconds and add a third set.*

**Coach's Tip:**

*Keep your knees straight, and walk on your heels without putting your toes on the floor.*

# PUSHUP [LIGHT + HARD DAY]

**Target Muscles:**

Chest, arms, core

**How-To:**

If you are new to strength training, start on your hands and knees. Place your hands a little more than shoulder-width apart so that when your arm is bent 90 degrees, your elbow is over your wrist. Keeping your core muscles contracted, push your body up and off the floor until your arms are extended; pause, slowly lower back down to just a little off the floor, and repeat.

**Progression:**

*Perform the pushup on your hands and toes. Even harder: Lift one foot off the floor.*

**Coach's Tip:**

*If you struggle with this exercise, try lowering your body back to the floor for a brief rest in between reps.*

## STANDING ROW + SQUAT [LIGHT + HARD DAY]

**Target Muscles:**

Back, arms, core, inner front of thighs

**How-To:**

Stand with your feet a little more than shoulder-width apart, toes pointed outward. Bend your knees 90 degrees and hold the position. Simultaneously, squeeze your shoulder blades together and pull back, bringing your elbows back behind you. Pause and return to starting position. Remain in squatting position for the whole set. Repeat.

**Progression:**

*Use a thicker tube, and squat every time you pull.*

**Coach's Tip:**

*Prior to pulling, squeeze your shoulder blades together, then pull, using your back muscles. Keep your torso tall, legs bent, and core muscles contracted.*

## SHOULDER RAISE [LIGHT + HARD DAY]

**Target Muscles:**

Shoulder stabilizers, upper back

**How-To:**

Lie facedown over a fitness ball so your back is flat and your chest is off the ball. Pull your shoulder blades into the center of your back (spine), moving your arms out to your sides, with your thumbs up and pointing to the ceiling.

**Progression:**

*Hold light dumbbells.*

**Coach's Tip:**

*Keep your head in line with your body, and focus on squeezing your shoulder blades together.*

# PLANK [HARD DAY]

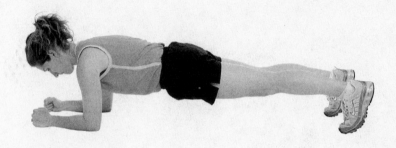

**Target Muscles:**

Core stabilizers, shoulders, hips

**How-To:**

Lie facedown with your forearms on the floor. Push up so your elbows are under your shoulders and arms are bent at 90 degrees. Hold your body in a straight line from your head to your feet. Hold this position for 15 to 20 seconds, then lower to rest. Repeat 4 to 6 times.

**Progression:**

*Hold the position 30 to 60 seconds for 5 to 8 reps.*

**Coach's Tip:**

*Focus on squeezing your buttocks, drawing your navel into your spine, and maintaining consistent breathing throughout.*

# CORE CRUNCH [LIGHT + HARD DAY]

**Target Muscles:**

Core

**How-To:**

Lie on your back on a stability ball with your hands behind your head and elbows out to the sides, like airplane wings. Crunch your rib cage toward your hips, focusing on keeping your arms at your sides and using your core muscles to perform the movement. Return to starting position.

**Progression:**

*Move your body back so more of your upper body is off the ball. With straight arms, hold a weighted medicine ball or weight over your chest.*

**Coach's Tip:**

*Focus on only one thing: moving your rib cage toward your hips. It is a small movement and, when done correctly, very effective. Avoid using your arms to lift and keep them at your sides (unless you are holding a weight). If you feel this in your back, move your body forward on the ball for more support.*

## CORE TWIST WITH TUBE [HARD DAY]

**Target Muscles**

Core (obliques), shoulders

**How-To:**

Attach one end of a resistance tube to a stable object at shoulder height. Holding the tube handle, stand with your feet hip-width apart, arms straight out and toward the anchor point. Drawing your navel into your spine, use your core to twist your body as far as you can, keeping your arms straight and at shoulder height. Pause briefly, then return to the starting position. Repeat.

**Progression:**

*Move farther away from where the tube is anchored, stretching the tube.
Even harder: Use a thicker tube.*

**Coach's Tip:**

*Pretend there is a pole running straight through the center of your body and
rotate around it. Start and finish the twist with your core muscles.*

## COACH JENNY'S TIPS AND TRICKS

✓ Perform two or three strength sessions per week to strengthen your
  muscles, tendons, and joints—it's like building a concrete foundation
  for your house.

✓ Include exercises for your upper and lower body and core muscle groups.
  Strength and balance will improve form and efficiency.

✓ Invest in a few sessions with a trainer or physical therapist to learn
  proper form.

✓ Focus on technique, which is more important than the amount of weight
  you lift.

✓ Increase the resistance or add an element of balance when an exercise
  gets easy. Like your runs, these sessions should be challenging.

✓ Perform strength workouts no more than every other day to give your
  muscles time to heal.

✓ If you are new to strength training or haven't done it in a while, start with
  the light exercises for 8 weeks and progress to including both the light
  and hard moves.

# 15

# RUN YOUR BUTT OFF

## PENGUIN PEARLS OF WISDOM

*It's clear to me now that I'll never have a runner's body, no matter how many miles I run. Instead, I'm concentrating on having a runner's soul.*

It sounds crazy now, but I actually thought that when I started running, my body would dramatically change. I thought my legs would get longer, my hips more narrow, and my whole physique would be that of an elite athlete.

But my body is still my body. Where an elite athlete's body goes up, mine goes out. Where an elite athlete's body is vertical, mine is horizontal. My body looks like it was assembled from some genetic junk pile.

And yet it is the body that has carried me to more than 40 marathon finish lines. It is the body that has held my son and my grandchildren. It is the body that I have, and I am grateful for it.

An old running buddy of ours, Roy Benson, used to tell the story about how easy it is to lose weight. He would go into great detail about how you burn fat at low effort levels and carbohydrates at higher effort levels.

He explained that your body burns the highest percentage of fat, as a part of the total energy source, while you are sleeping. So, explained Roy, the most effective way to lose weight and burn fat is to—repeat after me—sleep your butt off.

Of course he was being facetious, but there was a grain of truth in his words. He recognized that for most new runners, the number one goal is not running a fast 5-K or marathon. The number one reason people start running is to lose weight.

And why shouldn't they? Why wouldn't the average person simply assume that all runners look like the skinny little runners you see on television during the Olympics? They're runners. They're skinny. Therefore, running must make you skinny.

It's what the logic experts call a false syllogism. You know:

> *All dogs have teeth.*
> *John has teeth.*
> *Therefore, John is a dog.*

In our syllogism:

> *Some runners are skinny.*
> *You are a runner.*
> *You might be skinny.*

Running to lose weight is as good a reason as any to start running; it's just not the only reason to start nor the only reason to stay with it.

We were going to write the shortest book on health and fitness ever written. We wanted to charge a lot of money for the book, even though it was only two sentences long. Sadly, we couldn't find a publisher willing to take that risk.

The title of the proposed book was actually longer than the book itself: *John and Jenny's No-Nonsense Guide to Substantial Weight Loss and Sustainable Weight Management: A Comprehensive Approach.* The book, in its entirety read:

**Eat less. Move more.**

The truth of the matter is that for about 90 percent of us, that's all there is to it. Are you gaining weight? *Eat less. Move more.* Do you want to lose weight? *Eat less. Move more.* Just had a baby and want to lose the pregnancy weight? *Eat less. Move more.* Beer belly starting to bother you? *Eat less. Move more.*

No publisher would take the book because everyone wants weight loss, weight management, and nutrition to be complicated and impossible to understand. If you don't believe me, walk through the diet and nutrition section of any major bookstore.

Here's what we know for sure: Carbs are good. Carbs are bad. Protein is good, except when it's bad. And fat is always bad, except when it's good.

We have both tried nearly every diet and nutritional magic pill that has come down the pike. The problem with nearly every diet or nutritional magic pill is that it only works for a little while, and then you have to get back to living your life.

Movement, though—running and walking in particular—*is* a magic pill. It's just a magic pill that takes 30 minutes a day, three or four times a week, to swallow. And it's a magic pill that only works if you keep taking it for the rest of your life.

We'd like a show of hands (and if you're reading this on an airplane, it is especially important that you actually raise your hand). How many of you would rather be *thin* than fit? Raise your hand.

How many of you would choose to be thin rather than fit for the rest of your life? Raise your hand.

If you were in a room filled with new runners, you'd see nearly every hand in the air. All of us still make the mistake of believing that being thin is better than being fit.

On the surface, John looks like a poster child for running as a weight loss strategy. After all, he lost 100 pounds before a doctor told him he needed to put 20 to 30 back on. Sure, losing weight was an important part of becoming more active at the beginning. But losing weight won't keep you out there running for the rest of your life.

So, what *is* the best way to lose weight and keep it off? Why, a combination of a healthy diet and running and walking, of course. They're efficient. They're doable. They're accessible to nearly everyone. They're fun. And here's how it works.

Let's talk about calories for a minute. A calorie is an expression of the amount of energy it takes to move a certain amount of weight over a certain distance and, to a degree, the amount of time. The amount of calories burned in any situation is a function of weight, distance, and time.

The average 150-pound person burns about 100 calories moving that 150 pounds the distance of 1 mile. So, to burn 100 calories, all that person has to do is move that 150 pounds 1 mile. A pound of body fat is equal to 3,500 calories. So, for every 35 miles run, he or she burns approximately 1 pound.

Keep in mind that these are estimates and not exact numbers. If you weigh more, you will burn more. If you weigh less, you will burn less. A 200-pound person will burn more calories covering 3 miles than a 100-pound person will because it takes more energy to move more weight.

So why run when you can walk and still burn calories? Because running gets you from point A to point B in less time and at a higher intensity, and it burns more calories than walking the same distance. If you have 40 minutes to exercise, in that time you can run or run-walk 3 to 4 miles or walk 2 miles. See what we mean? One is not better or more fun than the other. It's not that walking is bad and running is good. However, if you are looking for ways to lose weight and boost your metabolism, incorporating running with walking or running continuously will get you there quicker and with more calories burned.

In Chapter 2, we mentioned our good friend and elite runner Daniel. Daniel, when he's pushing, runs at faster than a 5-minute-per-mile pace. That's 12 miles, or 1,200 calories, per hour. So if Daniel were to run only 5 hours a week at that pace, he'd burn 6,000 calories a week. That would be nearly 2 pounds per week of body fat. Is it any wonder that Daniel can eat nearly anything he wants and still be thin?

But most of us are not like Daniel. Most of us are lucky to be running a 10-minute pace, so we're going to burn about 600 calories an hour, or 3,000 calories, in a 5-hour running week. That's not even 1 pound per week. And if you're like us and are running and walking at even slower paces, the amount of calories burned is even less.

On the flip side, though, if you made no changes to your eating habits—if you just kept eating and drinking the way you are today and walked or ran just 9 miles per week—you would lose about a pound per month. That's 12 pounds by next year at this time without having to give up a thing.

That is the key to losing weight and keeping it off. Reaching a healthy weight is a function not only of what goes out but also what goes in. Some of our running buddies like to joke that "we run, therefore we eat." Yes, it is true, we can eat a little more than if we weren't running, but it is also true that we can actually consume beyond the calories burned in running and gain weight!

The danger is overestimating the amount of calories burned and underestimating the amount of calories consumed. It's not fair. We know that. It can take an hour to burn 400 calories. You can *eat* 400 calories in less than a minute!

The key to successful long-term, lifetime weight loss and weight management is a balance between how active you are willing and able to be and how, what, and how much you're willing to eat. For us, that has meant finding both an eating strategy and an activity strategy and then blending them together to create a permanent, sustainable eating-and-activity routine.

I am often asked how, as a 43-year-old smoking, drinking, overeating man, I managed to lose weight. I wish I were smart enough to write a really good answer. I can't. So I'll just tell you the truth.

First off, I did start moving more. That wasn't hard because up until then, I wasn't moving at all. So for me, adding small amounts of bicycling—at first—and ultimately walking and running were the first steps toward weight loss.

Beyond that, though, I did make some rather dramatic changes both in how I ate and what I ate. My food trigger is sugar. The ups and downs caused by the huge insulin swings in my system were making me crazy. As best I could, I tried to eliminate sugar from my diet.

But more important, for more than 5 years, I measured every ounce of food I put into my body. Every ounce. I had no idea what a serving size was. I had no idea what a serving of breakfast cereal looked like. I can tell you, though, it isn't a large, overflowing bowl.

I weighed my food. All of it. I never guessed. I never "figured" that something was "about" 4 ounces. It either was or it wasn't.

In time, after those 5 years or so, I began to have a better handle on food proportion and serving size. I still have to be careful. It's easy enough to look at one of those giant bagels and convince myself that it's only one serving, even though I know it isn't.

Time for a little honest sharing: Jenny and I love ice cream. There are times when one of us will look at the other and say, "There must be ice cream in my life soon." There's just no getting around it. We are going to have ice cream. There's no sense telling ourselves that in order to live an active, healthy lifestyle, we must give up ice cream for the rest of our lives. It's not going to happen. It's just not worth it.

So don't tell yourself that being a runner means giving up all the foods you love. It doesn't. It does mean using some good judgment about amounts of food. No one really needs to eat a burrito as big as his head. But everyone probably does need to eat a burrito from time to time.

What does a successful diet, nutrition, and activity program for weight loss and improved running performance look like? That's not as easy a question to answer as you might think. We can give you some general guidelines, but ultimately you will have to find the recipe that's right for you. Some things to be aware of:

1. **Watch for empty calories that you mindlessly consume.** For some, this is the morning can of pop (or soda, depending on where you live). For others, it is that doughnut screaming your name in the break room. Be aware of what you're putting in your mouth. It's going to go somewhere. And chances are, it'll go to your waist or hips.

2. **Be aware of portion size.** Use smaller plates at home; when eating out, ask to be served a portion on a smaller plate and the rest in a to-go container. A restaurant in Chicago serves a huge bowl of pasta and calls it a single serving. We measured one. Each bowl is actually 17 servings. Enjoy foods that taste good, but avoid treating every meal like it is the Last Supper!

3. **Start your day with a balanced breakfast.** It breaks the fast, giving your body fuel to run on all morning, and increases your blood

sugar levels to avoid sugar cravings. Breakfast is important. Make the time for a healthful one.

**4. Include healthy snacks throughout the day and between meals.** Your blood sugar level sinks to the ground when you go several hours without eating, which makes you feel tired and run-down. For all-day energy, avoid skipping meals, and don't let yourself get hungry. Eat smaller portions every 3 to 4 hours. Carry healthy snacks with you to avoid grabbing empty-calorie foods at the last minute. Avoid the sugary foods that cause blood sugar levels to spike and then drop abruptly.

**5. Watch for persistent low-level eating—popcorn at the movies, potato chips in front of the television.** The tendency is to eat until the bag is empty. Pour your portion into a small bowl, then close the bag and put it away.

**6. Know your food triggers.** For some, it's sugar. For others, it's grease. If John has a doughnut in the morning, you can almost guarantee he's going to be looking for that sugar high all day long. For our friend Pete, once he gets going on the fatty fried foods, there's no stopping. It's a lot easier to avoid your trigger foods in the first place than to stop eating them once you've started.

**7. Get the good foods in first.** We all know we should be eating a colorful plate of foods: vegetables, fruits, grains, and lean proteins. Follow the 80/20 rule. If 80 percent of the time you eat well-balanced meals, 20 percent of the time you can enjoy a treat.

**8. Think of food as fuel.** Power up with wholesome and balanced foods. Eat like an athlete. Keep your meals balanced, with 60 to 65 percent of your calories from complex carbs like whole grains, veggies, and fruits; 12 to 15 percent lean protein; and 20 percent or less fat. The meals will stay with you longer and reduce the risk of carbohydrate cravings.

**9. Make sure you can see your food. Broccoli is good.** Broccoli covered in hollandaise sauce? Not so good. Baked potatoes are good. Baked potatoes covered in sour cream or butter? Not so good.

**10. Be aware of your fantasy food myths like these:** Broken cookies have no calories. Food eaten while standing has no calories. Food eaten off someone else's plate has no calories. You know what we mean!

**11. Figure out what triggers your desire for food.** What are you using food as a substitute for? Do you eat more when you are alone? When you are traveling? When you are with friends or family?

**12. Stay hydrated.** Our bodies consist of about 70 percent water, a percentage that's important to maintain. Incorporate water in your diet and include hydrating foods like fruits and vegetables. Do remember that overdosing on water is not only possible but can be just as dangerous as underhydration. You know you are well hydrated when your urine looks like lemonade, pale yellow in color. If it is dark yellow, you need to hydrate more. If it is clear, you are drinking too much.

**13. Remember that every day is a day to start over.** Making poor food choices one day does not doom you to a life of gluttony. If you make a mistake, admit it, learn from it, and let it go.

No one knows you better than you know yourself. No one can tell you what's best. No one can tell you what you can't eat or what you must eat. You have to figure that out for yourself.

And if all else fails, remember the text from our famous unpublished book.

Eat less. Move more!


## COACH JENNY'S TIPS AND TRICKS

✓ Avoid skipping meals. It will almost always result in eating poor-quality foods, performing poorly, and experiencing cravings. Be prepared and organized nutritionally. You will eat better and feel better.

✓ Keep a daily inventory of what you eat. I find that this helps to better identify where to make dietary changes. There are a variety of effective ways to track your fuel and activity. Online logs are incredibly useful tools; you can track your foods and activity and analyze the difference. What is going in? What's the percentage of carbs, protein, and fat? How many calories are you burning? Whether you want to eat better to improve performance or lose weight, knowing what you're eating is the first step. When I did this, I admit that it seemed a little tedious at first, but I soon became keenly aware of what I was putting in my body and what I needed to change.

✓ Remember that it takes 21 days to create a habit. If you change one aspect about your eating every 3 weeks and then move on to something else, those changes become habits, just like brushing your teeth. For example, add one green vegetable to your fuel log every day. But avoid trying to change everything at once. If you did this with exercise, you wouldn't be able to move the next day!

✓ Identify your food needs based on your activity levels. Some of us have 10-gallon tanks, while others hold 15. If we try to put 15 gallons in 10-gallon tanks, our bodies end up storing that extra fuel as fat.

✓ Beware of strict diets. Our bodies are well equipped to survive for days without food. We would need water before we food if we were stranded in a desert. If you skip meals, it signals to your body that it isn't going to have food, and your metabolism screeches to a halt. And if you continually go on and off diets, they stop working. Long term, dieting drastically decreases metabolism and makes body systems highly inefficient. If you have gone on and off diets for years, you may need a good year to boost your metabolism to a normal rate. Be patient with yourself, and make small changes over time. It is a less daunting, more successful strategy. Remember, there is always room for the treats—just not every day.

# 16

# LOOK BETTER, RUN BETTER

It was once said that running is an inexpensive sport. That may have been true in the '70s and '80s, but it certainly isn't true now. There are the basics like shoes, technical apparel, and sports bras that are a must, but there are also endless opportunities to spend money on the sport of running. We should know; our closets are full of the latest, greatest running tech toys and trick apparel.

# NAVIGATING THE FOOTWEAR DEPARTMENT

The well-dressed runner needs to build his or her wardrobe from the ground up, starting with the shoes. The right pair will help prevent injuries and support you mile after mile. Proper running shoes are more than footwear—they're the most important equipment a runner has. That's why there's so much to consider when running-shoe shopping.

## FITTING YOUR FEET

As you learned in Chapter 9, knowing what kind of arch you have is the first step in making a decision about a shoe. Shoes fall generally into a few large categories, but don't worry about what a shoe is called or what category the manufacturer puts it in. Concern yourself only with your needs.

The most basic shoe is called a *neutral shoe*. This is, on the whole, the shoe on the lower end of the price scale and the one with the fewest bells and whistles. That doesn't mean it's a bad shoe. In fact, basic neutral shoes might be the best shoe for you. A higher price doesn't guarantee a better shoe.

A neutral shoe usually has a midsole of just one color. Typically, that would be white. If you have a neutral foot with a normal arch, it's quite possible that you can get away with wearing a very neutral shoe. In fact, a word of caution: Never buy more shoe than you need!

Shoes with a little support on the medial (inside) of the midsole are called *stability shoes*. Probably 75 percent of all runners and walkers can get by with a decent pair of stability shoes. Again, just because one brand calls a shoe a *stability shoe* doesn't mean it will necessarily fit *you* like one. It has to feel right on *your* foot.

Stability shoes usually have a two-colored midsole. The outer edge is usually white, and the inner edge, beginning at or just inside the heel, is usually a deep gray. Different shoe companies use different materials, but the results are the same. Stability shoes keep your feet from moving inward (or pronating) too much or too fast.

The most stable shoes are called *motion control*. They are designed to control the inward motion of the foot as you go through the running or walking movement. In addition to the denser midsole material you'll find in a stability shoe, a motion control shoe will have something else to prevent your foot from rolling inward. This might be a plastic bridge at the arch or hunks of plastic in the inner heel. It doesn't matter. All the systems have the same goal.

The least stable shoes are called *cushioned shoes*. They feel great in the store and taking a few steps down the sidewalk. You'll feel like you've put pillows on your feet. It's tempting to believe that the cushioning is what you want and need. For nearly all of us, the highly cushioned shoe is an invitation to injury because it offers minimal support for the parts of your foot that experience the most impact.

What distinguishes one shoe company from the other is mostly the material or system that provides the cushioning, stability, and control—air, thermal plastic, or gel. Most shoe companies offer a complete line of shoes, offering something for everyone. The best shoe is the one that supports your foot optimally and feels comfortable.

## FINDING THE PERFECT FIT

Running and walking shoes shouldn't even have sizes on them. Not only do the manufacturers not agree among themselves as to what a size 9 is, they don't even agree within their own lines. So don't ask for the size you've worn since high school and think it will work. It won't.

You also can't choose a running shoe based on its overall length.

The adage "If the shoe fits, wear it" has no place in a long-distance running program. The critical measurement is not the overall length of the shoe but the length of the arch—the distance between the heel and the ball of the foot.

Your running shoe has to fit your arch, not your foot. Some of us (John) have long arches and short toes. The result was that he bought the wrong size shoes for nearly 5 years. The danger in having the wrong size is that the shoe won't articulate or bend at the same place your foot does.

Shoe width is also a consideration. If, like John, you've got duck feet, you'll need to find shoes that are wide enough through the ball of the foot to accommodate your foot. You'll also need to consider the "volume" of your foot. If you've got a thick foot, top to bottom, you'll need a shoe with enough room in the toe box to allow your foot to move without blistering.

The best way to determine which shoe is best for you is to shop at a local running specialty store where the staff is trained to fit you with shoes that match your foot type and running style. It's worth the investment of time and money. The running store professional should ask you how often you run, how long you've been running, if you have injuries or aches and pains during or after runs, and if you are training for an event. If you have shoes you've used only for running, bring them to the store. They are a good reference for what you've used and how the shoe wore.

The staff should fit you in a variety of shoes and watch you run in them to see if the shoe is properly supporting you. You may find several brands that work for you. Go with the one that feels the best. Let it be known now, you should not buy your shoes by color! Just because a pair matches your new running outfit doesn't mean it will match your foot type.

Shoes, like tires on a car, wear out in time. The outsoles lose their tread, the midsole loses its cushioning and stability, and even the uppers lose their shape and form. When? We can't say for sure. At the outside, even the best shoe won't last more than 6 months. At the first sign of a new ache or pain, assume it's your shoes, and replace them immediately. Keep track of the miles put on your shoes in your log. That way, you can determine just how many miles you can get per pair of shoes.

## REPLACEMENT INSOLES AND ORTHOTICS

One of the worst-kept secrets in the running and walking shoe industry is that you will pay $150 for a pair of shoes with the latest technology and still get a 15-cent insole or sock liner. No shoe company seems willing to invest in quality insoles. There are a few exceptions, but on the whole, even great shoes have lousy insoles.

Fortunately, there are a number of excellent options available in the over-the-counter or trim-to-fit insole market. Good products from Superfeet and other companies can be found at most running specialty and outdoor stores. These can be an excellent way of transforming a very good shoe into the perfect shoe.

Insoles are not a way to extend the life of a pair of shoes, however. The materials in the shoes are going to wear out regardless. Sticking a pair of soft insoles in a worn-out pair of shoes is a recipe for disaster.

## SORTING OUT SOCKS

Let's start with the only absolute rule about socks: Cotton kills. That favorite pair of cotton tube socks your kids gave you for your birthday might be fine for a casual softball game, but they will tear your feet to shreds while running.

Some people like thick socks. Thorlos and SmartWool, for example, offer an entire line of socks that are well padded at the heel and toe. Others of us like very thin socks. Companies such as DeFeet, Nike, and Balga make an excellent line of thin socks. There are even toe socks from Injinji that look like something out of *Mork & Mindy*. They look funny, but trail runners love them because they prevent blisters on toes.

## THE WOMEN'S DEPARTMENT: SPORTS BRAS

Guys, we need to talk girl stuff for a minute. Never underestimate the power of a support system. I remember back in the early '80s, sports bras were something you designated. The old bras were sports bras: You could sweat in them and not worry about ruining them. Need I mention they really didn't work that well? It wasn't until I tried my first real sports bra that I understood why I needed one, although even that first one needed some help. I called it the "unibra" because it was as technical as wrapping an ace bandage around your breasts. We've come a long way. Today, there are a variety of bras to match your exercise intensity, from low impact to high. The higher the impact level of your sport, the more support you'll need.

Try on different styles to find out what you like best. A good sports bra should feel comfortable, stay in place, and not chafe. The straps should not dig into your shoulders, and the band around your lower chest should not shift or bind.

Do jumping jacks, run in place, and swing your arms side to side to make sure that what feels good in the dressing room is also comfortable and supportive when you're in motion. Keep in mind that to provide support, a good sports bra should fit more snugly than a lingerie bra, but it should not restrict movement or breathing.

Look for breathable synthetic fabrics like Coolmax that wick moisture away from the skin and have a gently supportive stretch;

they also help to minimize chafing. Stay away from cotton and any sports bra with a zipper or rough seams. Although stylish, it has the potential to chafe and come unzipped.

There are basically two types of sports bras: the pullover, aka the uniboob, and the back clasp. Pullover bras are usually for runners with A and B cups. For larger cup sizes, pullovers will only be supportive enough for lower-impact exercises such as walking or spinning. Back-clasp sports bras generally come in C, D, and DD cups from 32 to 44. They also have adjustable shoulder straps to accommodate various cup sizes and volumes.

Statistics show that many women wear the wrong size sports bra. Following is a guide for measuring the right size sports bra. Use a cloth dressmaker's tape measure while wearing a regular lingerie bra (not a sports bra) that you think fits well.

1. Measure snugly around your rib cage, just underneath your breasts. Be sure the tape measure lays flat and even all the way around, not lower in the front or back.

2. Add 3 inches to your rib cage measurement, and you'll have your band measurement size.

3. Now measure around the fullest part of your bust, keeping the tape measure straight all the way around your body.

4. Subtract your band measurement from your breast measurement—the difference determines your cup size.

| Difference | Cup Size |
|------------|----------|
| 1 in | A |
| 2 in | B |
| 3 in | C |
| 4 in | D |
| 5 in | DD |

Once you find the right sports bra, it is important to take proper care of it. Wash it on a gentle cycle, and always hang it to dry. Machine drying breaks down the elasticity and support of the material.

## GET A LEG UP ON SHORTS AND TIGHTS

Let's start with the only absolute rule about chafing: Anything that rubs will chafe. John's battle with "chub rub" is well documented. Even if he puts on a layer of lubricant as thick as cake frosting, his thighs are creating sparks before the end of the first mile.

The two general categories of shorts are traditional running shorts and compression (or bike) shorts. Deciding which style to wear is mostly a matter of personal preference, your level of modesty, and the aforementioned dreaded chafing.

The advantage of traditional running shorts (and manufacturers have learned that not all of us want our cheeks hanging out and are making styles with longer inseams) is that they tend to be cooler and therefore more comfortable. Modern pairs have a wicking brief and microfiber outer short. Good ones aren't cheap, but they're worth every penny if they keep you comfortable on your runs.

The advantage of compression shorts is that they eliminate the chafing issue. They can also provide some measure of support for your thighs. For some of us, they are not all that flattering. I'm pretty sure that whoever invented spandex didn't have hip, butt, and thigh issues.

The question that never gets answered because no one is willing to ask it is, what do you wear under compression shorts? The answer isn't shocking. Some people wear nothing. Others wear some kind of brief. Wear whatever makes you comfortable.

One solution to the shorts controversy is to wear both. Some runners, like John, take an old pair of running shorts and cut out the liner, then wear those shorts over a pair of compression shorts.

Jenny prefers something a little more "flattering" with flowers or cute patterns. She sat down with the bigwigs from Nike and told them women want something longer to cover the hips and thighs but still look good. They responded, as did many other companies, and now there are lots of shorts from which to choose. Comfort and function still come first, but now we have a great selection. After all, what is training without great outfits?

When to move from shorts to tights is also a very personal decision. It can be pretty cold outside before your legs will get chilled during a long run or walk. More often then not, you'll be better off in shorts. Your body core temperature will increase as you run and make the outdoor temperature feel 15° to 20°F warmer than it is.

Like shorts, running tights come in all types. There are tight-fitting tights and loose-fitting tights; tights that wick and pants that block the wind. For most runs, a comfortable pair of wicking tights made of Dri-FIT or Drylete will do the trick. John prefers the loose-fitting tights, while Jenny likes the tight tights, adding a pair of wind pants when the temperature drops below 30 and windchill is a factor. The extra layer blocks the wind and keeps her legs warm.

## TOPS AND JACKETS THAT FIT TO A TEE

The three categories of tops are singlets (sleeveless), short-sleeved, and long-sleeved. As with socks, the only rule is: Cotton kills. Your favorite T-shirt is not the perfect training shirt. The right apparel will have a huge impact on the comfort of your runs.

Each manufacturer has its own name for its technical fabric, such as Dri-FIT or Drylete, but it's just a way of saying that the material is a polyester-based fabric designed to wick moisture away from the body. This wicking is important in hot *and* cold weather. In heat, you want the sweat away from your skin and out on the surface of the material, where it can dry. In the cold, you want the sweat moved away from your skin and onto the outermost layer, so you'll stay warm and dry.

Your personal taste and modesty will dictate what kind of top makes you most comfortable. With the technical fabrics, there really isn't much difference between a singlet and a short-sleeved shirt. The best option comes down to what you feel you look best wearing.

The decision regarding when to wear a long-sleeved technical shirt is a bit like the question about when to wear tights. It's based on your level of comfort and tolerance for cold. John tends to wear long-sleeved shirts even in temperate weather because it's what makes him comfortable. The key is to experiment with your clothes during your training and make notes in your log so you dial in your running apparel for various weather conditions.

Technical running jackets are made of wind- and waterproof yet breathable materials. Their main purpose is to keep out the wind, rain, and snow and "breathe" so moisture doesn't build up inside. A good running jacket will last several years (unless a cuter style comes along).

Every winter Jenny talks a few more new runners into running outdoors through the cold season. At first they look at her like she's crazy, but once they're acquainted with technical pieces like jackets, tights, and tops and how little they need to wear to stay warm, they're sold.

## HATS, HEADBANDS, AND MORE

Running through winter requires a hat or headband depending on your body, the windchill, and the temperature. In the coldest days, wear a fleece or wicking hat to avoid loosing precious heat through your head.

Grandma was right. She would yell to us as we headed out to sled, "Cover your head or you'll be cold!" She didn't know you can lose up to 40 percent of your body heat through your head, but she did know hats would keep us warm. If you don't wear a hat, your body will have to shift gears to keep you warm rather than focus on moving you forward.

Everyone has a different internal thermometer. Jenny puts on her headband at 40°F and a fleece hat when it is 35°F. John is warm-blooded and wears one only when it drops below 35°F. Hats keep you warmer and are geared to the colder temperatures, while headbands cover only your ears and work best in cool temperatures. If you live in a cold climate or will be racing in one, find out what your temperature gauge is and wear a hat or headband when needed.

For the coldest days, you can wear a neck gator or balaclava, which covers your head and neck and looks like something out of a Batman movie. You may look a little weird, but you will avoid getting a frozen face.

Technical running hats look like baseball caps but are made of fabrics that keep your head cool on warmer runs. They're great for rainy days and can also protect your head and face from the sun.

You can always tell the elite runners at a cold race. They are the ones racing in shorts, a singlet, and *gloves*! It could be 25°F, but they all wear the same thing: shorts, singlet, and gloves. Gloves and mittens are vital for winter running. A simple pair of gloves made of wicking materials will do the trick. Jenny prefers mittens as a wind barrier because her hands get very cold when she runs.

- - - - - - - - - - - - - - - - - - - - - - - - - - - - - - - - - -

## JENNY'S KEYS TO LAYERING

Dressing for cold-weather workouts can be confusing. The best way to go about it is to dress in layers. That way, if you get overheated, you can shed a layer and keep moving.

It's easy to overdress on those first fews days of cold weather. I remember the first cold day of one winter training program in which I coached new runners. It was 45°F, and everyone stood before me ready for a severe winter storm in hats, gloves, and big bulky jackets. Everyone had overdressed, and within the first mile, layers were coming off and flying all over the path.

One easy way to determine whether you are overdressed is to use the "out the door" test. Dress so you are chilled when you walk out the door for your workout. If you are warm before you begin, you will be too hot and risk overheating during the workout. You don't need to wear as much as you may think. Typically, you should dress for 15° to 20° warmer than the current temperature; that will account for your increased body temperature while moving.

- - - - - - - - - - - - - - - - - - - - - - - - - - - - - - - - - -

## ACCESSORIZE

It is true. Running can be an inexpensive sport: a pair of good-fitting shoes, socks, a sports bra, a top, and a pair of shorts, and you're ready to go. But if you want to accessorize, these extras might be of interest.

### THE BASIC WATCH

At some point in your running career, you will want a running watch. They're not very expensive, and they come with a variety of features.

If you're running and walking, a watch that has at least two interval timers is useful. The magic is that you can set the timers to your run interval ratios and push start. The alarm will go off at each interval so you know when to run and walk. Beyond that, look for a watch that has a chronograph to track overall running time, lap/split to track mile times, and a large number display you can see when you run.

## HEART RATE MONITORS

Heart rate monitors measure your heart rate. Tricky, huh? They come with a strap that goes around your torso and a watch that goes on your wrist. The chest strap sends a signal wirelessly to the watch, giving you instant feedback from your heart. Heart rate monitors are valuable training tools for a runner—especially for the runners who love numbers.

There are more heart rate monitors than ever out there. Manufacturers like Polar, Nike, and Timex make a variety, from the most basic model that tells you nothing more than that you are alive and that your heart is beating to one with all the bells and whistles, which will tell you your heart rate, your pace, your distance, and when you should call home to say hi.

The right model monitor is a very personal choice. If you are not interested in all the technical wizardry, then there's no sense spending the extra money. If you like being distracted by an array of data, there's no reason not to step up into one of the top-of-the-line models.

Then again, you could be like me and not be able to choose. I have two monitors that I use on a regular basis. One is a near-basic model that does nothing more than allow me to set my upper and lower limits and beeps at me. The other has a pod that goes on my shoe to tell me how far and how fast I'm moving, plus a heart rate monitor so that I can compare my pace with my effort.

## SPEED DISTANCE MONITORS

The first day I strapped on my speed/distance monitor, I felt like the kid in school with a brand new bike. A speed distance monitor (SDM) tells you your current running pace, distance, time, and even calories expended. It is by far the most fun running toy out there.

Gone are the days of driving your running course to see how far you've gone. There is no need to break out the calculator to figure out your pace. SDMs give you instant running feedback. You can alter your speed as you go. No more waiting to reach a mile marker to see how fast you are going—using an SDM tells you stride for stride. You can effectively learn how to correlate effort with speed and pace yourself. An SDM is an excellent training tool and the perfect running gadget for tech geeks like us.

Some SDMs work with shoe sensors that need calibration. The sensor measures the motion of your foot and translates it to the watch to show speed and distance. Other models use the Global Positioning System (GPS) to track miles and speed from above. Some are even auditory, so you hear your pace and distance along with your favorite tunes. As if that wasn't enough, you can download your training information to an online log and track your progress run to run. Need I say more?

## HYDRATION PACKS

Hydration is important for runs lasting longer than 45 minutes. You can bring your fluids with you in a hydration pack. Some come with several smaller bottles, which is nice; you can put a sports drink in one and water in another. Other packs include one bottle. If you are running for an hour or more and don't have access to fluids on the course, it's wise to train with a hydration pack.

## BODYGLIDE

This is a must-have for the runner who has chafing issues like John and Jenny. You rub Bodyglide on like deodorant, and it provides a lubricating layer to prevent friction and chafing.

# RUNNING SAFELY

It is important to be visible and carry ID when you run. There's a variety of reflective vests and lights you can wear to be visible on the roads when it's dark. Most running shoes and apparel are reflective as well. John and Jenny use head and tail lights for extra caution. It is also a good idea to have identification on you. Road ID makes runner-friendly ID tags that fit on your shoes. Not only are they informational and easy to find, they're also unobtrusive and won't get in your way!

## COACH JENNY'S TIPS AND TRICKS

✓ Start with a pair of well-fitting running shoes, socks, and technical apparel.

✓ Track the miles you put on your shoes and replace them every 350 to 500 miles or when they show signs of breaking down.

✓ Consider trail shoes if you run off-road or on uneven terrain. They provide extra traction and durability.

✓ Pass on racing flats at this point; they're meant for elite or very fast runners who are used to running with little or no support, cushioning, or stability.

✓ Wear your running shoes only when running.

✓ Wear water- and windproof, breathable apparel in the colder months and lightweight, light-colored, breathable apparel in the warmer months.

✓ Lube up. What can chafe will chafe.

# SECTION V

## RUNNING FOR YOUR LIFE

# 17

# BECOMING YOUR OWN COACH

Okay . . . You know your personal history and where you are fitness-wise. You know how the body works and that you need to be patient to become a runner. You know what to eat to fuel your body for performance and even lose weight. You know how to stretch to prevent injuries and the exercises to strengthen your foundation so you can run for a lifetime. Now it is time to talk training. Which program should you follow, how should you get started, and how should you progress?

As a running coach, I've developed lots of specialized training programs. This chapter explains the 12 separate and unique programs for getting started with your running career. There are five programs geared toward learning to run or even participating in your first 5-K (3.1 miles). There are four 10-K training programs that show you how to train for running an hour or more and three programs to run for weight loss.

The programs are developed progressively so that as you complete one, you can advance into the next. Let's say you begin with the 5-K Walk-Run Training Program. When you finish the 10 weeks of training required for this program, you'll be able to progress to the 5-K Run-Walk so that you can shift the balance of your workout more toward running. You could also make the decision to follow the 10-K Walk-Run Training Program so that you cover more mileage per workout. You may find you love the program you chose just as it is and decide not to switch things up. That's okay too. The nice thing about these programs is that they are very flexible and totally doable for the mortal runner. Any way you do it, you'll have fun. That's a guarantee.

The 5-K programs are developed for those who are new to running and want to train to run or run-walk 30 minutes three or four times per week. You can use the program simply to learn to run, or you can use it to train for your first 5-K; the decision is completely yours. Either way, by the end of 10 weeks, you will be moving for 30-plus minutes several times per week. And that's what counts!

The 10-K programs continue where the 5-K ones leave off. They progress in distance and frequency while preparing you to run or run-walk 60 minutes or more. This is the logical next step after the 5-K program and a great way to build your running mileage too. It will also prepare you to run a 10-K (6.2 miles).

The weight loss programs are geared toward those who want to combine running with losing weight. The mileage is lower but the frequency is higher. As a coach, I've found that most runners who get out there more frequently during the week and really keep track of what they eat lose the most weight.

Many runners believe marathoning is the best way to take off the pounds, but that is just not true. This is mostly because running marathons requires you to refuel for proper recovery. The result is that you end up being hungry most of the day.

The other key to successful weight loss and running is using a great program like Weight Watchers, in which you are accountable week to week for keeping track of your calories in and out. Several of my running clients have lost 25 to over 100 pounds using the combination of running and Weight Watchers. This is a great match and a successful strategy. It is hard to lose weight by just cutting calories. It's also a challenge to lose weight with exercise alone. Together, running and a balanced diet are the dynamic duo. The bonus of this strategy is that it teaches you how to balance eating and running for the rest of your life.

The program schedules read Monday to Sunday and are designed to train specific muscles and the cardiovascular system sequentially. Training days are strategically mixed with days of rest and cross-training to allow for optimal adaptation and recovery. Therefore, the sequence of workouts day to day is just as important as the intensity and duration. If you need to modify your workouts, it is very important to maintain their order day to day. The workouts can be moved, but it's crucial that you maintain their sequence.

I've spent many hours moving around workouts for runners and walkers to fit their busy lifestyles. You may find completing your longer workout is easier midweek because you work on weekends. You may need to switch the run workouts from one day to the next. And that's okay, as long as you keep the sequence.

The programs progress safely over time, so you are never at risk for doing too much too soon. The key to success is to follow the program and avoid adding to it because you are excited. This is especially true for all you type A runners. The quickest way to injury is by adding to these programs.

Of course, everyone will adapt differently. The trick is to identify the best program to begin with and listen to your body. As we mentioned earlier, you need to start by evaluating where you are *now* in terms of your goals to determine where you want to be in the future. You may start with the 5-K Run-Walk Training Program and find that in week 2, your body is aching all over. What does this mean? Most likely, the run-walk is too demanding, and you need to begin with the walk-run instead.

For all those folks who are exercising regularly but not yet running, good for you! Welcome to the running world. Remember, though, that just because you are fit and doing other activities doesn't necessarily mean you can successfully start with a run program. It is all about adapting to the impact of the forces of running. Your cardiovascular system is raring to go, but your muscles, tendons, and joints need to start from the beginning.

Now is the time to sit down with the results of the Personal Inventory Form you completed in Chapter 3 and match them up with the program that makes the most sense for you. Although this may sound easy, there are many variables to review while making the decision. To help you in the process, we've outlined a few participant inventories and the training programs they are using. All you have to do is match your personal inventory with one of the following participants.

# 5-K WALK TRAINING PROGRAM

## MEET LYNN . . .

Lynn was full of excitement and motivation to learn to run. She desperately wanted to run a local 5-K to benefit the American Cancer Society—that is, until we looked over her health history and fitness regimen. She was honest in admitting she hadn't worked out in years and that the last time she had, it was sporadic at best. Lynn is 45 years old, with a history of back and knee pain. I told her the inventory was more common than not and that there was a way we could strategically modify her goals.

Lynn humbly began with the 5-K Walk Training Program and has already completed her first 5-K. She has progressed to the Walk-Run 5-K Training Program and plans to participate in another charity 5-K in the future. Her goal is to continue through the run-walk program and eventually train with the run program so she can run the entire 5-K distance. She is well on her way because she started out slowly and wisely.

You may need to start at a different place than you might have guessed. That is okay because in the end, you, like Lynn, will progress without sabotaging your success—or your body.

The Walk Training Program is a perfect place to start if you have a history of injury, are a few pounds overweight, or have been inactive for months. You may want to walk because you enjoy the sport. You may also choose to walk as a means to running. Either way, walking is a good starting point.

# WALK-RUN TRAINING PROGRAMS

## MEET BOB . . .

Bob has been walking three or four times per week for 30 minutes for the past 10 months without injury or pain, but now he's getting low on motivation. He loves the benefits of walking but wants to add variety and challenge himself more. That is why he decided to register and train for two races: a 5-K and a 10-K. Bob doesn't necessarily want to run continuously, but he wants to make his workouts more challenging with a combination of walking and running. He's tried to run, but each time his efforts resulted in heavy breathing, frustration, and a few choice words.

Bob is 50 years old and healthy, with a solid base of walking minutes under his belt. He could focus on speed walking, but he wants to work on sprinkling running into his regimen for something different. We both agreed the 5-K Walk-Run Training Program is the best place for him to start.

Bob is currently 6 weeks into the walk-run program and loves it. It is the best of both worlds; it's challenging and includes a higher ratio of walking minutes than running. He is highly motivated and progressing nicely. Bob is looking forward to completing the 5-K and will do so with the smart walk-running system. His plan is to continue on with the 10-K Walk-Run Training Program and increase his mileage, speed, and distance.

This program is a great strategy for walkers who are eager to try running. It can also serve as a progressive program for walkers who want to improve their speed or add an element of challenge. Walk-running is an enjoyable way to train and race. It is mentally stimulating because you have to alternate throughout the duration, and it develops a great supporting cast of walking and running musculature. It also burns more calories than walking!

# RUN-WALK TRAINING PROGRAMS

## MEET JILL . . .

Jill has been running consistently for about 6 months, three times per week, for 35 to 40 minutes. She set a goal to run a 10-K.

Jill is 38 years old and about 10 pounds overweight. She has an on-and-off relationship with knee pain and is trying to come back after having a baby 8 months ago. Her main goal is to progress in distance to run the race but also have enough energy for her new daughter. She finds that her energy is running low after her runs, and she can't get beyond the 40-minute mark.

After a long heart-to-heart with Jill, I convinced her to train with the 10-K Run/Walk Training Program. She has the base to start with this, but her body needs a little less intensity when she trains. The run-walk is perfect for her. It incorporates power-walk breaks every few minutes of running to dial down the intensity and allow her body to recover run to run. The program leaves her invigorated and feeling strong rather than worn out and ragged. Run-walking has also helped her lose weight more easily because she was able to complete the workouts without pain, increase her time beyond 40 minutes, and run faster too.

Jill finished the 10-K, is injury-free, lost the baby weight, and still uses the run-walk program to train. She finds it provides enough challenge without the fatigue factor for this busy time in her life.

The run-walk programs offer a more forgiving regimen for running. The walking minutes provide a useful mental strategy and break the distance into smaller, more digestible pieces. This is John's personal training method, and I use it as well. Walkers, when they want to progress beyond the walk-run, can use the program to integrate more running into their regimen, and runners can use it to safely increase distance over time. It is a perfect blend and the hottest way to run these days.

# RUN TRAINING PROGRAMS

## MEET SUE . . .

Sue runs four times a week on a treadmill at work for stress relief and to maintain her weight. Some buddies at work challenged Sue to run a 10-K before her 40th birthday, which is a little over 2 months away.

Sue is in good health but has never run more than 45 minutes in a single workout. Her entire running career has been inside on a treadmill and at the same speed—10 minutes per mile.

Since Sue has a good running base, the 10-K Run Training Program is best for her to reach her goals. Sue is eager to get started but worried about running outdoors, especially since she reviewed the program and saw the longer endurance workouts on the weekend. We talked it over and came up with a compromise that would allow her to continue to train on a treadmill for the sake of convenience for some workouts, while exploring the great outdoors for the others.

Sue quickly realized that although running on a treadmill is beneficial, it is not as challenging as running outdoors. The weather and terrain are great challenges, and it takes more effort to move over the road than a tread. She trained indoors during the week and outdoors for the endurance workout. This prepared her for racing outdoors in the 10-K.

Sue is a smart runner. She was willing to modify her lifestyle and put in extra time on weekends to implement her new approach. Because of her efforts, Sue is now running 5 to 6 miles outdoors every weekend and is ready to race that 10-K on her 40th birthday.

The run training programs are ideal for those who have been running two or three times per week. The 5-K Run Training Program is great for those who are tackling 20 to 25 minutes, two or three times per week, while the 10-K Run Training Program is best for those who are running three or four times per week for 30 to 45 minutes. It offers a consistent progression of miles and cross-training to get you to the finish line running strong and injury-free.

# ADVANCED RUN TRAINING PROGRAMS

### MEET SHANNON . . .

Shannon runs several 5-Ks per year and has set a goal to improve her finish time. Shannon is 30 years old, has always been active playing sports and running, and has rarely been injured.

Although Shannon runs many 5-K races, she isn't pleased with her finish times. She has been running four or five times per week for 40 to 50 minutes but always at the same pace. She is great on consistency but doesn't vary her workouts much, making her a perfect candidate for the 5-K Advanced Run Training Program. She has the base of miles and benefits greatly from the speed workouts included in this program.

After following the program, Shannon ran a PR (personal record) for a 5-K and took over 3 minutes off her best time. She loves the challenge of the advanced speed sessions, and her body has adapted well to the program. She has set a new goal to race a 10-K and will use the advanced 10-K program to prepare.

It took patience, but she had an open mind and followed a different regimen. It required more of her physically, but it paid off on race day. She also found her competitive side and enjoys pushing a little harder in her training and racing.

The 5-K and 10-K Advanced Run Training Programs are perfect for those running regularly who want to step it up and improve their performance. It is important to note that, to avoid injury, you must have a strong base of running before following an advanced program.

Make sure you regularly run for 40 to 60 minutes at least four times per week before beginning these programs.

You'll notice the programs all include cross-training and rest days. It is the recipe of running plus cross-training plus rest that makes the happy runner. Strength training should also be included in the mix and can be done on the run days or cross-training days.

The balance of the program components makes the recipe a success. If you mess with the ingredients, the balance is off, and the meal tastes too spicy or too bland. These program recipes have just the right amount of spice without going overboard, so you can lead an active and healthy life.

Achieving a goal starts with a realistic plan. Oftentimes, a goal is set, but the plan for reaching it is too demanding. Begin with a realistic program for reaching a realistic goal based on your health history, and progress from there.

With this in mind, if you find yourself struggling to complete the training workouts, you are most likely using a program that is too difficult. That doesn't mean you can never train with that program; it simply means you will need to prepare with a different one to get to where you want to go. Anyone can beat his body to a pulp, but it takes wisdom, patience, and discipline—and the right program—to challenge your body without going overboard. Listen to your body, follow a realistic program, and day by day, your body will reward you by running farther with ease.

## WEIGHT LOSS PROGRAMS

### MEET BILL . . .

Bill has been exercising on and off for 3 years. He has struggled with his weight since he was young and has managed to lose more than 20 pounds with exercise. His doctor wants him to continue the program but also incorporate a healthy eating plan to lose another 25 pounds.

Since Bill was exercising by walking and strength training three days per week, we decided the best program for him would be the Weight Loss Program: Phase 1. This will have Bill walking more frequently while continuing his strength training. The eventual goal is to increase the intensity to walk-running.

The increase in frequency will rev up his metabolism every day rather than every other day, which will burn more calories and stoke his overall metabolism. Training almost every day will improve his spirits and motivation while keeping him on target for his goals.

He also agreed to join Weight Watchers and has pinpointed several foods that were getting in the way of further weight loss. Bill is in week 6 of the Phase I/Weight Watchers combination plan and has successfully lost over 8 pounds. He is feeling stronger and beginning to sprinkle running into his regimen.

Bill's success is due to his patience and tenacity. He is changing the way he eats, not just what he eats. He is making lifestyle changes and exercising more frequently. Eating healthfully and being active are a way of life now. That is the secret to weight loss, my friends. Slow and steady sheds the pounds.

## COACH JENNY'S TIPS AND TRICKS

✓ Understand the difference between running for recreation and following a training program: The former is optional, the latter is not. Training adds structure to your running and allows you to progress in fitness and performance.

✓ Know when to push and when to rest. Some days will go like clockwork, and others require a Plan B. Becoming your own coach takes patience, tenacity, and understanding. It all starts with being in tune with where you are now and where you want to go on your journey.

# 18
# RUNNING THE RACE

## PENGUIN PEARLS OF WISDOM

*It took years before running became a source of joy instead of frustration for me. It wasn't until I began to understand that ultimately my running matters only to me that I was free to run for myself.*

Running legend George Sheehan wrote that the difference between a jogger and a runner is the signature on a race application. For George, racing was the ultimate expression of the art of running.

In those days, races were the final exams. They were the tests you took to see if your training was working, to see if your body was ready, if your will was strong.

Today, races are celebrations. They are the expression of hope and joy and overcoming. They are where we discover that we are not on this journey alone.

## JOHN'S STORY

I guess I'd been running for 6 months or so when a friend asked me if I'd like to do a race. Remember that it had taken me all of those 6 months to get to the point of running and walking 3 miles, so the idea of racing was the farthest thing from my mind. Then he said that there weren't any pure running events the weekend he had in mind, but he had found a duathlon. I had no idea what a duathlon was except it sounded a little like that Olympic sport where they cross-country ski and then shoot. It didn't sound like me.

My friend explained that a duathlon was a run-bike-run event. For this particular duathlon, we would have to run a 5-K, then bike a 25-K, then run another 5-K. Don't forget, I had just run 3 miles for the first time in my life. Of course I said I'd do it!

My thinking was—and I know now how dumb this seems—that since I knew I could get through the first 3.1 miles, I'd be able to relax on the bike and rest up for the second 5-K. Honestly, that's what I thought.

We got to the race site, and I can tell you that I was more excited than I had been in years. Here were all these people with bikes and cool shoes and gear bags. It was, for me, like being at the Olympics. I took my bike down, rolled it to the registration table, got my running number and bike sticker, and headed to the transition area.

You must know by now that I had no idea what the transition area was or what we were transitioning into, but I went dutifully down there and found a place to hang my bicycle. Imagine my surprise when I realized that mine was the only bicycle there with a luggage rack!

They called the runners to their marks, and I made my way to the front row. After all, I had been running for 6 months; I had improved my mile time from nearly 30 minutes to something right around a 12-minute pace. I was ready to race. And when my friend Lee explained that I was competing only with men my age, I was sure there was a trophy in my future. After all, how could any 44-year-old man run faster than a 12-minute pace?

I was about to find out.

Fortunately for me, Lee dragged me to the back of the pack for the start. The gun went off, and the crowd disappeared. I couldn't believe it. Everyone was gone. And getting further and further away . . . quickly.

I started my run filled with equal parts enthusiasm and naïveté, which, as it turns out, is a pretty good combination for a first race. We were the last to finish the opening 5-K. Ours were the only bikes left in the transition area, and we set off on the bike leg.

By the time we were finishing the bike portion, many of the competitors were already on their way home. They would pass us as we were riding; they had their bikes back up on their cars and were headed out. We still had to run the final 5-K.

And we did. Slowly but surely, we made our way through those last 3.1 miles until, finally, we saw the finish line. It was a miracle—a finish line. My very first finish line.

I crossed the line dead last, arms raised in celebration, and I don't think I had ever been happier in my life. I had done it. I had raced a race. I had started and finished, and that was all that mattered.

That race was a long time ago, and yet I can still feel the hair on my arms stand up as I tell the story. I've gone on since to race hundreds of times, including more than 40 marathons, and I still think crossing that first finish line was the single most important moment of my life.

Something happens to all of us when we pin a number on our chests. Maybe it's the whole *Chariots of Fire* thing. Maybe we just start hearing that music in our heads and it transforms us. We go from being calm, easygoing people to full-on, full-throttle racers.

And make no mistake, the racing isn't just going on at the front of the pack. No way. There are monumental battles going on right where I am, inside of me. There are battles of wills, battles of egos, and challenges and counterchallenges as fierce as any you can imagine.

Where we are (at the back of the pack), it's all about the racing, pure and simple. We're not racing for position, and we're certainly not racing for money; we're racing only to satisfy our own need to race. We pass people and get passed by people in the most elegant athletic ballet possible.

We back-of-the-packers are warriors of the first order. We will hunt down a competitor for hours. I've chased young men, old men, young women, old women; it doesn't matter. If I see someone ahead of me that I don't think should be ahead of me, I'm going after them.

Woe to those who pass me in the latter stages of a race. I do not take kindly to being passed in the last few hundred yards. Do not challenge me! I assure you that you will be in for the fight of your life.

But when the race is over, we just fall into each other's arms and laugh. We laugh at the silliness of our own egos. We laugh at the weakness of our bodies and the strength of our wills. We laugh because we know that the difference between victory and defeat— for us—is just a state of mind.

But racing well is an art.

## COACH JENNY'S TAKE ON RACING

If you look up the word *race* in the dictionary, it says "a contest between or among runners to decide who is the fastest; a contest between two or more people seeking to do or reach the same thing, or do or reach it first." I've stood at enough finish lines to know that the definition of a running race goes well beyond the first finisher.

Not to take anything away from the talent it takes to finish in the top 10, but racing is more about doing your best than being the best or the first. What other sport in the world allows you to participate with the winner? Most of us can't golf with Tiger Woods or play baseball with the Cubs. We can, however, run a race with the winners. And that is what is so exciting about running a race. It rewards everyone from the first to the last.

There are a few things you need to realize. One, there are no style points in racing. There won't be people on the sidelines critiquing your form or telling you to move faster. There will be people, but they will be cheering for you!

Two, in most cases, you won't finish last. I thought the number one fear was public speaking until I began to talk to runners about racing. Everyone thinks he or she is going to finish last. If you let that fear get in your way, you will never reach that finish line or have the race shirt and bragging rights that go with it. If you are nervous about racing, volunteer for a race. It will give you a chance to see who is racing and how much fun they're having.

Participating in a race takes some thought and effort. It is best to start with a shorter race and, if you love it, build up the distance. For instance, train and race a 5-K before you tackle a marathon. You will learn something in every race and quickly develop your racing skills.

Follow a structured training regimen like the ones in this book. They will prepare you for the distance so you can enjoy the journey on race day. Training is preparation for the celebration.

Train at the same time that the race starts to get used to what it feels like to run at that time of day. If the race begins at 7:00 a.m., train at 7:00 a.m. a handful of times to see how your body reacts to early morning running. Training runs are dress rehearsals for the race.

Practice everything you will do on race day, from your prerace meal to hydrating. That way, there will be no surprises on race day. The general guideline is to consume 6 to 8 ounces of fluid during every 15 to 20 minutes of activity. This becomes more important as the race distance increases. For races of 45 minutes or less, water is optimal. For races 45 minutes or longer, it is recommended to use water and a sports drink like Gatorade.

Train using the sports drink the race is serving on the course to make sure it agrees with your system. Sports drinks are made to replenish lost energy and electrolytes. It is more important to get them in you rather than on you during the race. Walk through the aid station, look a volunteer in the eyes or point to him or her, and grab the cup. Pinch the cup, drink up, and go! It should take only a few seconds once practiced.

Prerace meals should be consumed 2 or more hours prior to the start of the race or training. A light meal containing 200 to 400 calories of food that's high in carbohydrates and low in fat, fiber, and protein is optimal. The less you weigh, the fewer calories you'll need. The meal will get into your system quickly and help fuel your performance.

Preferences for prerace meals vary. John does well with cereal and milk, and I go with toast and peanut butter. Take the time to figure out your ideal prerace meal.

Review the race course ahead of time. It will give you a chance to visualize the race and anticipate the mile markers, hills, and aid stations. Mentally rehearsing allows you to become more familiar with the course for race day.

Race week will feel a lot like your very first week of school. Remember the nerves, the fears, the crying? You will most likely have the emotional stability of a 5-year-old child. You will start questioning your training, worry about finishing, and might not be able to sleep. Don't worry; that is normal. I typically have nightmares about getting lost on the race course and ending up shopping at Nordstrom's. My point is that you may be nervous, and that is okay. It is good stress; it means you respect the distance, and it will be a challenge. The challenge is what motivates you to train and race. The challenge will keep you running for years.

Keep things familiar during race week. This is not the time to try a new cuisine or all-broccoli diet or power hydrate with water. Keep it simple and similar to what you normally do. Don't try anything new on race day. Wear the shoes you trained in as well as clothes you are familiar with. Avoid drinking sports drinks unless you've practiced doing so in training.

Pick up your race packet early—before the day of the race, if possible. A race packet typically includes a bib number, a race shirt, race information and directions, and a timing chip. The bib number identifies who you are on the course. The timing chip activates your time once you cross the starting line and stops when you cross the finish line. It's a great tool, especially if you are running a large race.

## A WORD ABOUT RACE SHIRTS

The race shirt proves to family and friends that you did it. It is a badge of honor. Now pay close attention here: The race shirt can be worn only if you complete the race. Wearing it before or during the race or even sleeping in it if you didn't run the race will bring you years of bad running karma. It is a running secret passed on through the years and an important rule to follow.

Place the chip on your shoe and bib number on your shirt the night before the race. The last thing you want to have to do race morning is figure out how to strap a small plastic piece on your shoe. You'll have enough to think about at that point.

Get to the race 1 hour before the start. This will give you time to use the Porta Potty, check your gear, warm up, and figure out where the race start is. Rushing around is a waste of energy and will take the joy out of the race.

At the starting line, position yourself with people who appear to have similar pace or ability. If you run an 11-minute pace and line up near the front with the 6-minute pace runners, you will go out way too fast and crash and burn very quickly. It is easy to get caught up in the excitement at the start of the race. Lining up appropriately will help keep you at the right speed for you.

Pace yourself wisely and invest in the last few miles. The number one variable you can control on race day is your pace. Learn how to use your watch to monitor your mile splits. That way you will know how to pace mile by mile and avoid a crash-and-burn at the end.

The most effective way to pace is to run either even splits or a negative split. Running even splits means running at a continuous pace that is neither too hard nor too easy. This works well for some runners and not so well for others. Even splits are great for seasoned runners who know their pace like the backs of their hands.

A negative split means running the first half of the race slightly slower than the second half. Running a negative is typically the best way to start your running career because it allows you to finish strong at the end. To run negative, start out slowly, about 10 to 20 seconds per mile slower than the planned pace for the second half. If you are planning to race a 5-K (3.1 miles) in 31:00, it works out to be a pace of 10:00. If you run the first 1.5 miles at 10:10 and the second half at 9:50, you average a 10:00 pace overall. This strategy conserves energy and strength for the final miles and allows you to play with various speeds without risking going too hard, and you will have fun passing runners in the end too!

Be flexible. You may train hard, then race day comes along and your performance ends up being less than what you thought it would be. You will have strong and poor race performances. Be prepared to learn from the tough ones. They teach us more than the strong runs do. Figure out what went wrong. What did you change? Was it your training or pacing or just the weather? Figure it out, and modify it for the next race.

Ultimately, it is all about the finish line photo. In large races, there will be a photographer waiting for you to finish. You want to look strong, not like you have just beaten yourself to a pulp. We even know a runner who takes the time to put on lipstick before the finish. Pace wisely, and smile for the camera.

When you cross the finish line, keep moving and let your body gradually come back to reality. Continue to walk for at least 5 minutes postrace. Drink a sports drink to replenish lost energy and electrolytes, and consume a meal high in complex carbohydrates and moderate in protein within 60 minutes of the finish.

We've watched thousands of runners cross finish lines. We've seen runners cry, hug each other, and shake their fists in the air. The finish line means something different for everyone. Race day is all about celebration. You will only finish your first race once. Enjoy the journey, and celebrate your achievements. It is the finish of this race but the start of your whole new life as a runner.

## COACH JENNY'S TIPS AND TRICKS

✓ Prepare yourself mentally. Training is 90 percent physical and 10 percent mental. Racing is 90 percent mental and 10 percent physical. Break up the race into smaller, more digestible pieces. Run mile to mile, or pick fun geographical markers on the course and set up mini finish lines. It is much easier to run several shorter distances than one long race from the start.

✓ Have faith in your training. A great race is the outcome of a strong training foundation. Review your training log. It will reinforce you and remind you of all the training and preparation.

✓ Use a splits bracelet to determine if you are on pace during the race. The bracelet is a band of paper that runners wear around their wrists to indicate what their time splits should be at different mileage points in the race. You can print one from a running Web site or create your own.

✓ Run the tangents on the race course. When you see a turn, run straight through it at a 45-degree angle rather than hugging the outside curve. A straight line is the shortest distance between two points.

✓ Recover from the race by taking 1 day for every mile of the race easy. If you ran a 5-K, take it easy the first 3 or 4 days postrace and either rest, cross-train, or run at a very easy pace. This will give your body time to recover from the intense effort of the race.

✓ Gradually increase your training after the race. Listen to your body for postrace aches and pains. The longer the race, the longer the recovery period.

✓ Reward yourself with a massage 4 or more hours after the race. A relaxing massage can speed the rate of healing and reduce postrace muscle soreness.

# 19

# LIVING WITHOUT LIMITS

For nearly all of us, the music we listen to becomes the soundtrack of our lives. There are songs and lyrics that become inextricably tied to a time and place, a person, or an event. This association becomes so strong that one can't exist without the other.

But even more than the music that's stored on the hard drives that are our psyches, there are thousands of memories scattered deep in our subconscious that alone and in concert control much of what we think about the world and, more important, what we think about ourselves.

Our perceptions of our abilities, our looks, and our intellects are really nothing more than tiny bits we've collected and stored over the course of our lives. For most of us, those bits of data are a hodge-podge of other people's opinions and beliefs. We collected them and stored them because we thought they were about us. They weren't. They were impressions of someone else's thoughts and beliefs. We took them on because we didn't have an alternative point of view.

Make no mistake. We were no different from you. I began elementary school at 5 years old and was always one of the youngest boys in my class—one of the smallest, least physically developed, and least athletic-looking. Jenny, although athletic as a child, was still haunted by the sharp contrast between her tomboy image and what a young woman was supposed to be.

These perceptions of what we are, what we're capable of, and what we think or even dare to attempt don't change just because we get older. If there is any reinforcing incident or idea, like not being a good baseball player or that being athletic is the antithesis of being feminine, then that becomes the center of a constellation of experiences that form our self-images.

You can change all that.

If you've made it this far in the book, then you may have already begun to make the change. If you didn't think you could be a runner when you picked up the book, we hope that by now you know you can. If you didn't think you were a runner when you picked up this book, we hope that by now you realize you are.

If you've spent your life believing that becoming an athlete was beyond you, then it's time you took a deep look at that belief, where it came from, and whether the validity of that belief makes any sense to you now.

The late George Sheehan, one of the running community's greatest philosophers, wrote that we are all athletes. Some of us are just in training and some of us are not. You may have spent your entire life as an athlete who was not in training. But that doesn't sentence you to a life of sedentary confinement.

To live without limits means, from our point of view, learning how to see beyond what is and catch a glimpse of what might be. More important, once you get good at looking beyond your self-imposed limits, you'll be able to look beyond what might be to what you never imagined. We know. It's happened for us both.

Jenny saw the Eco-Challenge on television. She saw coed teams of four hiking, paddling, mountain biking, and navigating for 8 to 10 days. She saw ordinary people achieving extra-ordinary feats of strength and courage. And for an instant, she saw herself among the competitors.

Two years later, she was standing at the starting line with her team at the Eco-Challenge Borneo, getting ready to spend the next 8 days in the Malaysian jungle.

I heard a friend talk about what it was like to run a marathon. I heard him tell about the trials and satisfaction that come from trying to complete a 26.2-mile event. A year and a half later, that same friend and I crossed the finish line of the Columbus Marathon.

It's not that either of us is particularly courageous. It's only that we've both learned that the limits we imposed on ourselves weren't *our* limits. They were limits based on the fears of parents, of friends and family, and of the people who loved us so much that they wanted us to stay who they believed we were.

You don't have to participate in the Eco-Challenge or run a marathon to live a life without limits. You can begin by identifying and facing your most fundamental fears about yourself, the consequences of failing, what you look like when you are fully you, and taking the first step.

# FEET, DON'T FAIL ME NOW

For most beginning runners, the thought of lining up in a race is terrifying. We're all sure that we will be last. We'll be so slow that we'll be asked to get off the course. We'll get so far behind the rest of the crowd that we'll get lost. We'll be so mortified that we'll have to move to a new town and change our names.

Well, if it makes you feel any better, I've experienced nearly all of that. I have been last. I have been asked to get off the course, and I have gotten so far behind that I got completely lost. And so what?

What's the shame in being last? Even the last-place finisher beat everyone who stayed home. Even the final finisher lined up at the start, ready to take on the challenge of the course and the day. Even the last finisher succeeded. Being last is simply that—being last.

The first step in living without limits is accepting that anything that happens in a race is actually quite insignificant when you look at the bigger picture. You can make it seem like a big deal. You can make it seem like the consequences are earth-shattering, but they aren't. The truth is, where you finish doesn't matter to anyone but you. And if you can get right with it, the rest of the world won't care.

What follows are some of our recommendations for things you can do, both right now and as your life as an athlete continues, to help you discover, as we did, that a life lived well and without limits is far better than one lived in fear.

# RUNNING

## FIRST STEP: THE 5-K

There are 5-K races nearly every weekend almost everywhere, from small local fundraisers for schools or hospitals to the huge Race for the Cure 5-Ks in most big cities. It doesn't matter whether it's 25,000 people or 75. The point is to be in it.

There are 5-K training programs out there too, including the ones in the back of this book. Pick a race, follow a program, and then, like any other athlete, make your plan and get to it.

The very act of committing to a race is usually motivation enough to train. The commitment is the same whether you're preparing for the Olympics or the Firecracker 5-K: You set a goal, you don't let yourself chicken out, and you do whatever is necessary to take a shot at achieving your goal.

Notice we didn't say that you *would* achieve your goal. You may. You may not. It doesn't matter. In a life without limits, it isn't achieving that matters, it's trying.

## THE NEXT STEP: MARATHONING FOR MORTALS

Reading this you may be thinking, *Right. I'm going to run or walk 13.1 or 26.2 miles.* We don't blame you for being skeptical. All we can say is that every year, hundreds of thousands of people just like you are getting medals for running half and full marathons.

The key is to find an event that celebrates effort as well as excellence. There are a number of races throughout the country that fit that description. Chief among them are the John Bingham Racing series of half marathons and the Elite Racing series of "musical" marathons and half marathons. For more information, check out the Web sites JohnBingham.com and EliteRacing.com.

Committing to a 14- to 20-week training program is not for the timid. You'll find that your life becomes neatly divided into the things you have to do because you're training and the things you can't do because you're training. You may even find that your running friends are the only friends you have left at the end of the program. We've found that nonrunners aren't all that interested in where we're getting blisters, and they have almost no interest at all in talking about chafing. Long-distance runners and walkers can't get enough of those conversations.

If the idea of training alone is too intimidating, find a local commercial training program. Better yet, join a local or national charity-training program. (John is the national spokesperson for the Leukemia and Lymphoma Society's Team in Training.) Many of us have found that knowing that the good we're doing for ourselves also benefits someone less fortunate doubles our joy and satisfaction.

## AND NOW FOR SOMETHING COMPLETELY DIFFERENT

**Go for a hike.** As a runner, even if you're new to it, you'll find that the world is accessible to you with your own two feet and bigger than you ever expected. And it's all within your reach.

One of our first adventures together was hiking the Na Pali Coast in Hawaii. For me, the fear of taking off on a narrow coastal trail with no end in sight was nearly paralyzing. Fortunately, Jenny was a gentle but insistent guide, and we made our way farther and farther down the trail. Since then, we've hiked the rain forest in Kuala Lumpur, the high desert of the American Southwest, and snowshoed in the Canadian Rockies.

**Run a relay race.** Running tends to be an individual sport. It's too easy to isolate yourself from the runners around you and become so wrapped up in your own running that you lose the sense of being a part of something beyond yourself. Running as a member of a relay team changes that.

The mother of all relays is the Hood to Coast Relay in Oregon. It begins near the summit of Mount Hood and continues for 200 miles out to the Oregon coast. The teams consist of 12 runners in two vans who take turns running. The teams are started in reverse-speed order. The slower teams begin early in the morning, with the faster teams beginning later in the day. We were members of a team that was so slow that every one of us was passed on every leg. For 32 hours we ran and were passed. But in the end we had found a way for our running to take us places that our feet could never go. We had run into the hearts and souls of our teammates.

# BEYOND RUNNING

## WHEELS OF FORTUNE

**Buy a bicycle.** Every runner ought to have a bicycle. It doesn't have to be fancy or expensive or have all the latest bells and whistles. It just has to have two wheels, a seat, handlebars, and pedals.

The experts will tell you that riding a bicycle is a good way to cross-train. And it is. But it's also just a lot of fun. As your aerobic capacity expands because you're a runner, you will discover that getting out and riding a couple of days a week is just as much fun now as it was when you were a kid.

We recommend a hybrid bike. The streets are filled with mountain bikes that never get dirty and road bikes that would be the envy of riders on the Tour de France. The truth is that a medium-tired bicycle with flat handlebars will get most of us through 90 percent of our riding needs.

**Want more?** Train for an organized ride. If you've begun to enjoy long-distance training and like the calm that comes from running for an hour or so at a time, you'll probably enjoy training for an organized cycling event. The most popular distances are the century (100 miles), metric century (62 miles), half century (50 miles), and half metric century (31 miles). If you really get into it, you may find that you need different or better equipment, but there are thousands of folks out there riding centuries on very inexpensive bicycles.

## UP A CREEK WITH A PADDLE

**Learn to kayak or canoe.** What's so great about running is that it is the perfect aerobic base for every other kind of activity. You may not always have the specific skills you need, but you'll have the strength and courage to get started.

It's only fair to tell you that my first kayak lesson wasn't exactly an unmitigated success. The instructor said something like "Try to get comfortable in the kayak," at which point I turned mine upside down. Other than a good soaking, there was no harm done, and it did give the instructor the opportunity to teach the rest of the class about rescue and recovery. But other than that one episode, life on the water has been all good. We recommend taking a class because there are some paddling skills for kayaking or canoeing that are best learned early.

For us, learning to paddle has allowed us to kayak in some of the most beautiful and exotic places on earth, including Resurrection Bay in Alaska, the calm rivers of Hawaii, and alongside whales in Antarctica.

## FINDING YOUR WAY

**Learn to orienteer:** In parts of the world outside of the United States, orienteering is a very popular sport. In its simplest form you have a map, a compass, some checkpoints you have to find, and that's about it. The faster you find the points, the better your score.

As a runner, you'll already possess the necessary physical skills for orienteering. What you'll need to learn are the map reading and compass skills. These shouldn't be underestimated. In the world of GPS (Global Positioning System) mapping, it feels nearly primal to be finding your way using compass points and bearings. And it feels great to find a checkpoint.

## PUTTING IT ALL TOGETHER

**Try an adventure race.** Once you've got biking, paddling, and orienteering skills, you might as well combine them and become an adventure racer. You don't need to start with a 10-day expedition-length race. There are plenty of fun 3- to 8-hour races.

Probably the most fun and challenging races—and doable ones—in a life without limits are the 24-hour races. It's daunting to think that you will be thinking, planning, moving, and adapting all day and all night long, but it is also an almost unimaginable rush to think that you can. Jenny, with three Eco-Challenges on her résumé, in addition to other expedition-length races and a host of 24-hour and multiday team and solo events, is an expert on the outer limits of adventure racing. But, in his own way, John—both as crew and as a racer—defines what the average person can do if he can get past his fear.

## LIVING WITHOUT LIMITS

What most of us discover as we accept the challenges we face as runners is that the lessons we learn with our own two feet are the ones we need most in living our lives. We learn, as only runners can learn, that life can only be lived one step at a time.

We learn that what seems impossible at first seems eminently possible as we carefully and persistently pursue our goals. We learn that the 3 miles we thought we could never run become the easy days in our later training.

We learn that our lives are not separated from our running. We come to see that the good days and bad days that we accept in our running are the same good days and bad days that we have to accept in our lives. We learn that the limits we impose on our imaginations are no more real in the rest of our lives than they were on our running life.

We learn to live in a world that is constantly changing and expanding. We learn that we can reach into ourselves and find everything we need.

We learn that we have something in common with runners of every age and gender and ability. We learn that we are among those who have chosen to take control of some small portion of their lives. We learn that every foot strike takes us farther from what we used to be and closer to where we *want* to be.

Finally, we learn that life is best lived in those moments of honest effort, when there is no separation between success and failure.

## COACH JENNY'S TIPS AND TRICKS

✓ Use your running fitness to branch out and try new activities. Running will give you the confidence to be adventurous.

✓ Realize that *fear* is a bad four-letter word. Tackle your fears one at a time. It will open up a whole new world of opportunity.

✓ Break out of the mold and run a race in another state or country. It is a great way to explore a city.

✓ Set a goal to try something new this year—trail-running, kayaking, cycling . . . It will freshen your running and brighten your life.

✓ Don't avoid trying something new because you can't imagine yourself, say, skydiving or scuba diving. But remember, you didn't think you could run, and now you're a runner. Imagine. Conquer. Explore.

# 20

# THE COURAGE TO START

*The miracle isn't that I finished.*
*The miracle is that I had the courage to start.*

CREDO OF JOHN "THE PENGUIN" BINGHAM

Those words were first written while I was riding in the backseat of a Dodge minivan on the way home from a half Ironman triathlon in

Panama City, Florida. The day before, I had swum 1.2 miles, bicycled 56, and run 13.1. The winners had finished in around 4 hours. I was out there nearly 8.

Those words spontaneously erupted from my soul and passed without filtering through my fingers and onto the keys of an old laptop. Originally, those words were never intended to be read by anyone but me. They were and still are the truest expression of how I feel when I complete an event. They are the words that I live by.

It was, indeed, a miracle. For someone who was then 46 years old, just a few years earlier had weighed 240 pounds (at 5 foot 8), had smoked for 25 years, overate as a way of life, and drank more than his fair share of alcohol, to be alive and fit was nothing short of a miracle.

There is a kind of grace that passes over those of us who have transformed our lives with our own two feet. That grace is available to you if you are open to it. The miracle is not something that you need to wait for. You can make it happen yourself.

The miracle is that you have everything you need to change your life at your disposal right now. You don't need to be any smarter or thinner or more disciplined than you are at this very moment in order to accept the grace that an active life gives you.

In my case, as I wrote, the miracle wasn't that I finished. I had prepared long and well for the event. I had put in the hours in the pool and on the road, swimming and biking and running. I had paid my dues. I lined up with the tools and training I needed to finish.

The miracle was that, at age 46, I had the courage to fill out the race application. The miracle is that I had the courage to load up my bike and drive to Florida. The miracle is that I locked away everything I had previously thought about myself and my abilities and showed up.

The miracle is that I had the audacity—the pure, blind nerve—to stand at the starting line in a Speedo and dive headfirst into the Gulf of Mexico.

I should tell you, in the spirit of full disclosure, that I wasn't exactly driven by some inner competitive urge. The truth is that about halfway through the swim portion of that race, I was just sort of floating facedown and looking at a school of fish beneath me when one of the organizers told me I really needed to keep swimming if I wanted to make the cutoff time.

The bike leg was a near disaster. A spoke broke on my rear wheel, and the wheel was so out of round that it scraped against the brake pads on both sides—even with the brakes in the open position.

The run was a lonely shuffle across concrete bridges and through deserted neighborhoods. Even the palm trees didn't make it seem exotic. It was just plain hard.

I finished to the sounds of silence, as the crowds of well-wishers and athletes had long since left. The clock was still ticking away, but that was about the only evidence that there had ever been a race that day.

Standing in the Gulf of Mexico again, more than 8 hours after I had begun the odyssey, I was stunned by how little I actually felt. There was no rush of emotion. No fist-pounding sense of having defeated some enemy. There was only the awareness that I had witnessed a miracle. I had—for that day at least—believed I was an athlete.

The miracle was that I had the courage to start.

Courage is often confused with the absence of fear. Fear—especially the fear of failing—is an ever-present emotion. I didn't stand at the starting line filled with confidence. I was filled with fear. The difference was that, for the first time in my life, I was controlling the fear. The fear wasn't controlling me.

The first step in finding the courage to start is identifying the fear that keeps you locked in place. What is it that is holding you back? What are you so afraid of that you can't imagine being without the fear?

Many of us are afraid to be something other than what we already are. That's no surprise. The people who love us the most are sometimes the same people who don't want us to change. They love us the way we are. If we want to be something else, it threatens them.

But as afraid as you may be to become someone else, as afraid as you might be about releasing yourself from the prison of sedentary confinement and living an active, healthy lifestyle, you can put that fear behind you. In fact, to discover what you are and what you might be, you will have to find a way to face the fear.

Most of us had the courage to explore, to discover, to wander aimlessly into the unknown when we were children. A young child has to be taught to be afraid. And there are things of which a child should be afraid. But failure isn't one of those things.

Children will stand and try to walk and fall on their butts over and over without fear of failure. They will take a few tentative steps, fall over, get up, and try again. Children are not afraid to fail. Children are afraid to accept that who they are right now is all they are going to be.

Do you have the courage of a child? Do you have the courage to fail? Are you more afraid that who you are is all you'll ever be than of the struggle to find out what you can be? If so, you are ready to be a penguin, just like me.

There is no failure so devastating as the fear of failure that we create in our own minds. When people tell me that they are disappointed with their results, I always ask, "Why? What difference would it have made if you had finished 5 minutes sooner than you did? What about the world would have been altered by your performance?"

Of course, they have no answer. They may give me a song and

dance about the satisfaction of taking on a personal challenge, about how rewarding it is to be better, about how the only real competition is with themselves. I just smile.

I know that somewhere just below the surface is a parent's voice or a sibling rivalry or some memory of a failure that has hardened in their souls. I know that their inability to be happy is as much a part of them as the color of their eyes.

It's difficult, I know, to believe that doing your best is all you need to do. It's difficult to believe that your best on any given day is all you have to give. It's difficult to believe that you are the only one who knows what your best is. It's difficult, but it's not impossible.

Beginning today, you can become your own best cheerleader. Beginning today, you can look at yourself as a flawed but hopeful character ready to embark on the adventure of a lifetime. Beginning today, you can find not only the courage to start but also the courage to change.

You can find the courage to embrace progress in whatever form it comes. You can learn to savor each small victory that every day presents, even if that victory is nothing more than walking out your door.

You can find the courage to celebrate your accomplishments even if you are the only one who knows what they are. You can learn to find joy in the simple act of trying.

The path that you've chosen is your own path. No one has walked it before you. No one is sneaking up behind you. You are on this journey by yourself. And you are all you'll ever need.

The miracle is that those two feet that have carried you every day of your life are now ready to take you places that you've never even dreamed of. They can take you deep into yourself and miles away from yourself all at the same time.

You were born to move. You were born to walk and run and

chase. You were born to be an athlete. No matter how far out of shape you think you are, there is still a road back. It may be long. It may be fraught with setbacks and frustrations, but it's there. All you need to do is take that first step. Take that one step toward a new you. Then take the next and the next.

I cannot tell you what lies ahead for you, just as I can't tell you what lies ahead for me. Life has to be lived moving forward and evaluated looking back.

What I can tell you is that the past is right where it's always been. It's behind you. All the sorrow, all the glory, and all the hope and pain that were there yesterday will be there tomorrow. You are in no danger of losing touch with what you've been.

But I can assure you that what lies ahead is brighter, more exciting, more fulfilling, and filled with more unmitigated joy if you are active than if you are sedentary.

And it is worth the effort.

Waddle on, friends.

# APPENDIX

# APPENDIX

## RUNNING FOR MORTALS 5-K WALK TRAINING PROGRAM

The 5-K Walk Training Program is best suited for those who want to walk a 5-K or have been inactive for 4 or more months.

| Day | Monday | Tuesday | Wednesday |
| --- | --- | --- | --- |
| MODE | Walk | Cross-train or Rest | Walk *Pickups |
| PACE OR INTENSITY | Conversational | Moderate | Conversational + Challenging |
| I-RATE SCALE | 6.5–7.5 | 6–7 | 7–8 |
| HEART RATE | 65–75% | 60–70% | 70–80% |
| WEEK 1 | 25 min | 30 min | 25 min |
| WEEK 2 | 25 min | 30 min | 25 min |
| WEEK 3 | 25 min | 30 min | 30 min |
| WEEK 4 | 30 min | 30 min | 30 min |
| WEEK 5 | 30 min | 30 min | 35 min *Pickups |
| WEEK 6 | 30 min | 30–40 min | 35 min *Pickups |
| WEEK 7 | 35 min | 30–40 min | 35 min *Pickups |
| WEEK 8 | 35 min | 30–40 min | 40 min *Pickups |
| WEEK 9 | 40 min | 30–40 min | 40 min *Pickups |
| WEEK 10 | 30 min | 30 min | 30 min *Pickups |
| POSTRACE WEEK | 35 min | 30 min | Rest |

Postrace is a perfect time to set another goal. If you want to maintain this program, continue repeating week 8. If you want to progress, consider walking a 10-K or following the 5-K Walk-Run Training Program.

### SCHEDULE KEY

*Walk workout*: Walk at a conversational pace (you can still talk) at an i-Rate level of 6–7 or, if you are using a heart rate monitor, at 60–70% of maximum heart rate. This pace should be one notch above your easy warmup pace or a level at which you are breathing a little more vigorously.

*\*Pickups:* Walk the workout at an easy pace and include three or four short, 30-second pickups. Pick up your pace to a challenging pace where you can hear your breathing and it feels just outside your comfort zone. This is NOT at all-out gut-wrenching pace, simply one more notch up from where you were walking. Keep the pickup to 30 seconds maximum. Your effort level should be 8 on the i-Rate level or 80% of maximum heart rate.

| | Thursday | Friday | Saturday | Sunday |
|---|---|---|---|---|
| | Rest Day | Cross-train or Rest | Walk | Rest Day |
| | | Moderate | Conversational | |
| | | 6.5–7.5 | 6–7 | |
| | | 65–75% | 60–70% | |
| | Rest | 30 min | 30 min | Rest |
| | Rest | 30 min | 30 min | Rest |
| | Rest | 30 min | 35 min | Rest |
| | Rest | 30 min | 35 min | Rest |
| | Rest | 30 min | 40 min | Rest |
| | Rest | 30–40 min | 40 min | Rest |
| | Rest | 30–40 min | 45 min | Rest |
| | Rest | 30–40 min | 50 min | Rest |
| | Rest | 30–40 min | 45 min | Rest |
| | Rest | 30 min | 5-K Walk | Rest |
| | Rest | 30 min | 40 min | Rest |

*Cross-training:* Include activities that are nonrunning or walking. If you are new to an active lifestyle and have been inactive, rest on the cross-training days for the first 4 weeks, and then add the cross-training workouts to the schedule for week 5. If you are active 3 or 4 days already, follow the schedule as it appears. Cycling, swimming, Pilates/yoga, strength training, elliptical training, stairclimbing, and Spinning are great cross-training modes for 5-K training. Cross-training allows you to rest your running muscles while training opposing muscle groups and reducing the risk of overtraining and injury. It helps speed recovery and reduces burnout. (See strength-training exercises in Chapter 14.) Cross-training activities should be done at a moderate pace at an i-Rate level of 6–7 or 60–70% of maximum heart rate.

## RUNNING FOR MORTALS 5-K WALK-RUN TRAINING PROGRAM

The 5-K Walk-Run Training Program is best suited for those who have been walking or exercising regularly two or three times per week for at least 3 to 4 months.

| Day | Monday | Tuesday | Wednesday |
|---|---|---|---|
| MODE | Walk-run | Cross-train or Rest | Walk-run |
| PACE OR INTENSITY | Conversational | Moderate | Conversational |
| I-RATE SCALE | 6.5–7.5 | 6–7 | 6.5–7.5 |
| HEART RATE | 65–75% | 60–70% | 65–75% |
| WEEK 1 | Run 1 min; walk 3 min. Repeat 6 times for a total of 24 min. | 30–40 min | Run 1 min; walk 3 min. Repeat 6 times for a total of 24 min. |
| WEEK 2 | Run 1 min; walk 3 min. Repeat 6 times for a total of 24 min. | 30–40 min | Run 1 min; walk 3 min. Repeat 6 times for a total of 24 min. |
| WEEK 3 | Run 1 min; walk 3 min. Repeat 6 times for a total of 24 min. | 30–40 min | Run 1 min; walk 3 min. Repeat 7 times for a total of 28 min. |
| WEEK 4 | Run 1 min; walk 3 min. Repeat 7 times for a total of 28 min. | 30–40 min | Run 1 min; walk 3 min. Repeat 7 times for a total of 28 min. |
| WEEK 5 | Run 1 min; walk 3 min. Repeat 7 times for a total of 28 min. | 30–40 min | Run 1 min; walk 3 min. Repeat 7 times for a total of 28 min. |
| WEEK 6 | Run 2 min; walk 3 min. Repeat 6 times for a total of 30 min. | 30–40 min | Run 2 min; walk 3 min. Repeat 6 times for a total of 30 min. |

| | Thursday | Friday | Saturday | Sunday |
|---|---|---|---|---|
| | **Rest Day** | **Cross-train or Rest** | **Walk-run** | **Rest Day** |
| | | Moderate | Conversational | |
| | | 6–7 | 6.5–7.5 | |
| | | 60–70% | 65–75% | |
| | Rest | 30–40 min | Run 1 min; walk 3 min. Repeat 6 times for a total of 24 min. | Rest |
| | Rest | 30–40 min | Run 1 min; walk 3 min. Repeat 6 times for a total of 24 min. | Rest |
| | Rest | 30–40 min | Run 1 min; walk 3 min. Repeat 7 times for a total of 28 min. | Rest |
| | Rest | 30–40 min | Run 1 min; walk 3 min. Repeat 7 times for a total of 28 min. | Rest |
| | Rest | 30–40 min | Run 2 min; walk 3 min. Repeat 6 times for a total of 30 min. | Rest |
| | Rest | 30–40 min | Run 2 min; walk 3 min. Repeat 7 times for a total of 35 min. | Rest |

(continued)

## RUNNING FOR MORTALS 5-K WALK-RUN TRAINING
## PROGRAM *(cont.)*

| Day | Monday | Tuesday | Wednesday |
|---|---|---|---|
| MODE | Walk-run | Cross-train or Rest | Walk-run |
| PACE OR INTENSITY | Conversational | Moderate | Conversational |
| WEEK 7 | Run 2 min; walk 3 min. Repeat 6 times for a total of 30 min. | 30–40 min | Run 2 min; walk 3 min. Repeat 7 times for a total of 35 min. |
| WEEK 8 | Run 2 min; walk 3 min. Repeat 7 times for a total of 35 min. | 30–40 min | Run 2 min; walk 2 min. Repeat 9 times for a total of 36 min. |
| WEEK 9 | Run 2 min; walk 2 min. Repeat 9 times for a total of 36 min. | 30–40 min | Run 2 min; walk 2 min. Repeat 9 times for a total of 36 min. |
| WEEK 10 | Run 2 min; walk 2 min. Repeat 9 times for a total of 36 min. | Rest | Run 2 min; walk 2 min. Repeat 8 times for a total of 32 min. |
| POSTRACE WEEK | Run 2 min; walk 2 min. Repeat 9 times for a total of 36 min. | Rest | Run 2 min; walk 2 min. Repeat 9 times for a total of 36 min. |

Postrace is a perfect time to set another goal. If you want to maintain this program, continue repeating week 8. If you want to progress to more running, follow the 5-K Run-Walk Training Program.

**SCHEDULE KEY**
*Walk-run workout*: After the warmup, walk 5 minutes at a brisk pace. Run at a conversational pace (you can still talk) for prescribed number of minutes, and follow with walking at a brisk pace for prescribed minutes. Example: Run 1 minute; walk 3 minutes. Repeat sequence six times for a total of 24 minutes.

| | Thursday | Friday | Saturday | Sunday |
|---|---|---|---|---|
| | **Rest Day** | **Cross-train or Rest** | **Walk-run** | **Rest Day** |
| | | Moderate | Conversational | |
| | Rest | 30–40 min | Run 2 min; walk 3 min. Repeat 8 times for a total of 40 min. | Rest |
| | Rest | 30–40 min | Run 2 min; walk 3 min. Repeat 8 times for a total of 40 min. | Rest |
| | Rest | 30–40 min | Run 2 min; walk 2 min. Repeat 10 times for a total of 40 min. | Rest |
| | 30 min | Rest | 5-K Race Run 2 min; walk 2 min. start to finish | Rest |
| | Rest | 30 min | Run 2 min; walk 2 min. Repeat 10 times for a total of 40 min. | Rest |

*Cross-training:* Include activities that are nonrunning or walking. If you are new to an active lifestyle and have been inactive, rest on the cross-training days for the first 4 weeks, and then add the cross-training workouts into the schedule for week 5. If you are active 3 or 4 days already, follow the schedule as it appears. Cycling, swimming, Pilates/yoga, strength training, elliptical training, stairclimbing, and Spinning are great cross-training modes for 5-K training. Cross-training allows you to rest your running muscles while training opposing muscle groups and reducing the risk of overtraining and injury. It helps speed recovery and reduces burnout. (See strength-training exercises in Chapter 14.) Cross-training activities should be done at a moderate pace at an i-Rate level of 6–7 or 60–70% of maximum heart rate.

## RUNNING FOR MORTALS 5-K RUN-WALK TRAINING PROGRAM

The 5-K Run-Walk Training Program is best suited for those running a first-time 5-K, those who have been running sporadically for a few months, or runners getting back into it after an injury.

| Day | Monday | Tuesday | Wednesday |
|---|---|---|---|
| MODE | Run-walk | Cross-train or Rest | Run-walk |
| PACE OR INTENSITY | Conversational | Moderate | |
| I-RATE SCALE | 6.5–7.5 | 6–7 | 6.5–7.5 |
| HEART RATE | 65–75% | 60–70% | 65–75% |
| WEEK 1 | Run 3 min; walk 2 min. Repeat 5 times for a total of 25 min. | 30–40 min | Run 3 min; walk 2 min. Repeat 5 times for a total of 25 min. |
| WEEK 2 | Run 3 min; walk 2 min. Repeat 5 times for a total of 25 min. | 30–40 min | Run 3 min; walk 2 min. Repeat 5 times for a total of 25 min. |
| WEEK 3 | Run 3 min; walk 2 min. Repeat 5 times for a total of 25 min. | 30–40 min | Run 3 min; walk 2 min. Repeat 6 times for a total of 30 min. |
| WEEK 4 | Run 3 min; walk 2 min. Repeat 6 times for a total of 30 min. | 30–40 min | Run 3 min; walk 2 min. Repeat 6 times for a total of 30 min. |
| WEEK 5 | Run 4 min; walk 2 min. Repeat 5 times for a total of 30 min. | 30–40 min | Run 4 min; walk 2 min. Repeat 5 times for a total of 30 min. |
| WEEK 6 | Run 4 min; walk 2 min. Repeat 5 times for a total of 30 min. | 30–40 min | Run 4 min; walk 2 min. Repeat 6 times for a total of 36 min. |

| Thursday | Friday | Saturday | Sunday |
|---|---|---|---|
| **Rest Day** | **Cross-train or Rest** | **Run-walk** | **Rest Day** |
| | Moderate | Conversational | |
| | 6–7 | 6.5–7.5 | |
| | 60–70% | 65–75% | |
| Rest | 30–40 min | Run 3 min; walk 2 min. Repeat 5 times for a total of 25 min. | Rest |
| Rest | 30–40 min | Run 3 min; walk 2 min. Repeat 5 times for a total of 25 min. | Rest |
| Rest | 30–40 min | Run 3 min; walk 2 min. Repeat 6 times for a total of 30 min. | Rest |
| Rest | 30–40 min | Run 3 min; walk 2 min. Repeat 6 times for a total of 30 min. | Rest |
| Rest | 30–40 min | Run 4 min; walk 2 min. Repeat 6 times for a total of 36 min. | Rest |
| Rest | 30–40 min | Run 4 min; walk 2 min. Repeat 6 times for a total of 36 min. | Rest |

*(continued)*

## RUNNING FOR MORTALS 5-K RUN-WALK TRAINING PROGRAM (cont.)

| Day | Monday | Tuesday | Wednesday |
|---|---|---|---|
| MODE | Run-walk | Cross-train or Rest | Run-walk |
| PACE OR INTENSITY | Conversational | Moderate | |
| WEEK 7 | Run 4 min; walk 2 min. Repeat 6 times for a total of 36 min. | 30–40 min | Run 4 min; walk 1 min. Repeat 7 times for a total of 35 min. |
| WEEK 8 | Run 4 min; walk 2 min. Repeat 6 times for a total of 36 min. | 30–40 min | Run 4 min; walk 1 min. Repeat 7 times for a total of 35 min. |
| WEEK 9 | Run 4 min; walk 1 min. Repeat 8 times for a total of 40 min. | 30–40 min | Run 5 min; walk 1 min. Repeat 7 times for a total of 42 min. |
| WEEK 10 | Run 5 min; walk 1 min. Repeat 5 times for a total of 30 min. | Rest | Run 5 min; walk 1 min. Repeat 5 times for a total of 30 min. |
| POSTRACE WEEK | Run 5 min; walk 1 min. Repeat 6 times for a total of 36 min. | Rest | Run 5 min; walk 1 min. Repeat 6 times for a total of 36 min. |

Postrace is a perfect time to set another goal. If you want to maintain this program, continue repeating week 8. If you want to run a 10-K, follow the 10-K Run-Walk Training Program.

### SCHEDULE KEY
**Run-walk workout**: After the warmup, walk 5 minutes at a brisk pace. Run at a conversational pace (you can still talk) for prescribed number of minutes and follow with walking at a brisk pace for prescribed minutes. Example: Run 3 minutes; walk 2 minutes. Repeat sequence five times for a total of 25 minutes.

| | Thursday | Friday | Saturday | Sunday |
|---|---|---|---|---|
| | **Rest Day** | **Cross-train or Rest** | **Run-walk** | **Rest Day** |
| | | **Moderate** | **Conversational** | |
| | Rest | 30–40 min | Run 4 min; walk 1 min. Repeat 8 times for a total of 40 min. | Rest |
| | Rest | 30–40 min | Run 4 min; walk 1 min. Repeat 8 times for a total of 40 min. | Rest |
| | Rest | 30–40 min | Run 5 min; walk 1 min. Repeat 7 times for a total of 42 min. | Rest |
| | Rest | Rest | 5-K Race Run 5 min; walk 1 min. start to finish | Rest |
| | Rest | 30 min | Run 5 min; walk 1 min. Repeat 7 times for a total of 42 min. | Rest |

*Cross-training:* Include activities that are nonrunning or walking. If you are new to an active lifestyle and have been inactive, rest on the cross-training days for the first 4 weeks, and then add the cross-training workouts into the schedule for week 5. If you are active 3 or 4 days already, follow the schedule as it appears. Cycling, swimming, Pilates/yoga, strength training, elliptical training, stairclimbing, and Spinning are great cross-training modes for 5-K training. Cross-training allows you to rest your running muscles while training opposing muscle groups and reducing the risk of overtraining and injury. It helps speed recovery and reduces burnout. (See strength-training exercises in Chapter 14.) Cross-training activities should be done at a moderate pace at an i-Rate level of 6–7 or 60–70% of maximum heart rate.

# RUNNING FOR MORTALS 5-K RUN TRAINING PROGRAM

The 5-K Run Training Program is best suited for those who have been running 20 to 30 minutes at least two or three times per week for at least 4 months.

| Day | Monday | Tuesday | Wednesday |
|---|---|---|---|
| MODE | Run | Cross-train or Rest | Run/Pickups* |
| PACE OR INTENSITY | Conversational | Moderate | Conversational + Challenging |
| I-RATE SCALE | 6.5–7.5 | 6–7 | 7–8 |
| HEART RATE | 65–75% | 60–70% | 70–80% |
| WEEK 1 | 25 min | 30–40 min | 25 min |
| WEEK 2 | 25 min | 30–40 min | 25 min |
| WEEK 3 | 25 min | 30–40 min | 30 min |
| WEEK 4 | 30 min | 30–40 min | 30 min |
| WEEK 5 | 30 min | 30–40 min | 35 min |
| WEEK 6 | 35 min | 30–40 min | 35 min |
| WEEK 7 | 35 min | 30–40 min | 40 min |
| WEEK 8 | 40 min | 30–40 min | 40 min |
| WEEK 9 | 40 min | 30–40 min | 35 min |
| WEEK 10 | 35 min | Rest | 30 min |
| POSTRACE WEEK | 35 min | 30 min | 35 min |

Postrace is a perfect time to set another goal. If you want to maintain this program, continue repeating week 8. If you want to run to improve your time, consider following the Advanced Run 5-K Training Program. If you want to run a 10-K, follow the 10-K Run Training Program.

## SCHEDULE KEY

**Run workout**: After the warmup, walk 5 minutes at a brisk pace. Run at a conversational pace (you can still talk) at an i-Rate level of 6–7 or, if you are using a heart rate monitor, at 65–75% of maximum heart rate.

***Pickups:*** Run the workout at an easy pace and include three or four short, 30-second pickups within the run. Pick up your pace to a challenging pace where you can hear your breathing and it feels just outside your comfort zone. This is NOT at all-out gut-wrenching pace, simply one more notch up from where you were running. Keep the pickup to 30 seconds maximum. Your effort level should be 8 on the i-Rate Scale or 80% of maximum heart rate.

| | Thursday | Friday | Saturday | Sunday |
|---|---|---|---|---|
| | Rest Day | Cross-train or Rest | Run | Rest Day |
| | | Moderate | Conversational | |
| | | 6–7 | 6.5–7.5 | |
| | | 60–70% | 65–75% | |
| | Rest | 30–40 min | 30 min | Rest |
| | Rest | 30–40 min | 30 min | Rest |
| | Rest | 30–40 min | 35 min | Rest |
| | Rest | 30–40 min | 35 min | Rest |
| | Rest | 30–40 min | 40 min | Rest |
| | Rest | 30–40 min | 40 min | Rest |
| | Rest | 30–40 min | 45 min | Rest |
| | Rest | 30–40 min | 45 min | Rest |
| | Rest | 30–40 min | 40 min | Rest |
| | Rest | Rest | 5-K Race | Rest |
| | Rest | 30 min | 40 min | Rest |

*Cross-training:* Include activities that are nonrunning or walking. If you are new to an active lifestyle and have been inactive, rest on the cross-training days for the first 4 weeks, and then add the cross-training workouts into the schedule for week 5. If you are active 3 or 4 days already, follow the schedule as it appears. Cycling, swimming, Pilates/yoga, strength training, elliptical training, stairclimbing, and Spinning are great cross-training modes for 5-K training. Cross-training allows you to rest your running muscles while training opposing muscle groups and reducing the risk of overtraining and injury. It helps speed recovery and reduces burnout. (See strength-training exercises in Chapter 14.) Cross-training activities should be done at a moderate pace at an i-Rate level of 6–7 or 60–70% of maximum heart rate.

# RUNNING FOR MORTALS 5-K ADVANCED RUN TRAINING PROGRAM

The 5-K Advanced Run Training Program is best suited for those who have been running 40–50 minutes at least four times per week for at least 1 year.

| Day | Monday | Tuesday | Wednesday |
|---|---|---|---|
| MODE | Run | Cross-train or Rest | Run |
| PACE OR INTENSITY | Conversational | Moderate | Challenging |
| I-RATE SCALE | 6.5–7.5 | 6–7 | 8–9 |
| HEART RATE | 65–75% | 60–70% | 80–90% |
| WEEK 1 | 40 min | 30–45 min | 45 min *Pickups |
| WEEK 2 | 40 min | 30–45 min | 45 min *Pickups |
| WEEK 3 | 40 min | 30–45 min | 45 min *Pickups |
| WEEK 4 | 45 min | 30–45 min | 45 min *Speed A workout |
| WEEK 5 | 45 min | 30–45 min | 45 min *Speed A workout |
| WEEK 6 | 45 min | 30–45 min | 45 min *Speed B workout |
| WEEK 7 | 45 min | 30–45 min | 45 min *Speed B workout |
| WEEK 8 | 45 min | 30–45 min | 45 min *Speed C workout |
| WEEK 9 | 45 min | 30–45 min | 45 min *Speed C workout |

| Thursday | Friday | Saturday | Sunday |
|---|---|---|---|
| Cross-train or Rest | Run | Run | Rest Day |
| Moderate | Conversational | Conversational | |
| 6–7 | 6.5–7.5 | 6.5–7.5 | |
| 60–70% | 65–75% | 65–75% | |
| 30–45 min | 40 min | 45 min | Rest |
| 30–45 min | 40 min | 45 min | Rest |
| 30–45 min | 40 min | 50 min | Rest |
| 30–45 min | 40 min | 50 min | Rest |
| 30–45 min | 40 min | 45 min | Rest |
| 30–45 min | 40 min | 60 min | Rest |
| 30–45 min | 40 min | 50 min | Rest |
| 30–45 min | 40 min | 60 min | Rest |
| 30–45 min | 40 min | 45 min | Rest |

*(continued)*

## RUNNING FOR MORTALS 5-K ADVANCED RUN
### TRAINING PROGRAM *(cont.)*

| Day | Monday | Tuesday | Wednesday |
|---|---|---|---|
| MODE | Run | Cross-train or Rest | Run |
| PACE OR INTENSITY | Conversational | Moderate | Challenging |
| WEEK 10 | 40 min | Rest | 40 min *Speed D workout |
| POSTRACE WEEK | 35 min | 30 min | 35 min |

Postrace is a perfect time to set another goal. If you want to maintain this program, continue repeating weeks 4–8. If you want to run a 10-K, follow the 10-K Advanced Run Training Program.

**SCHEDULE KEY**

*Advanced run workout*: After the warmup, walk 5 minutes at a brisk pace. Run at a conversational pace (you can still talk) at an i-Rate level of 6–7 or, if you are using a heart rate monitor, at 65–75% of maximum heart rate.

*Speed A workout:* After the warmup, walk 5 minutes at a brisk pace. Run 10 minutes at an easy pace. Then repeat the following five times: Run 1 minute hard at 85–90% of maximum heart rate or 8–9 on the i-Rate Scale, followed by running 3 minutes at an easy pace to recover. It is key to be disciplined and run the easy segments easy. Otherwise, the quality of your running and progressing is compromised. After the 1-minute repeats, run 5 minutes easy, then cool down.

*Speed B workout:* After the warmup, walk 5 minutes at a brisk pace. Run 5 minutes at an easy pace. Then repeat the following five times: Run 2 minutes hard at 85–90% of maximum heart rate or 8–9 on the i-Rate Scale, followed by running 3 minutes at an easy pace to recover. It is key to be disciplined and run the easy segments easy. Otherwise, the quality of your running and progressing is compromised. After the 2-minute repeats, run 5 minutes easy, then cool down.

*Speed C workout:* After the warmup, walk 5 minutes at a brisk pace. Run 5 minutes at an easy pace. Then repeat the following six times: Run 2 minutes hard at 85–90% maximum heart rate or 8–9 on the i-Rate Scale, followed by running 2 minutes at an easy pace to recover. It is key to be disciplined and run the easy segments easy. Otherwise, the quality of your running and progressing is compromised. After the 2-minute repeats, run 5 minutes easy, then cool down.

| Thursday | Friday | Saturday | Sunday |
|---|---|---|---|
| Cross-train or Rest | Run | Run | Rest Day |
| Moderate | Conversational | Conversational | |
| Rest | 30 min | 5-K Race | Rest |
| Rest | 30 min | 40 min | Rest |

*Speed D workout:* After the warmup, walk 5 minutes at a brisk pace. Run 10 minutes at an easy pace. Then repeat the following four times: Run 1 minute hard at 85–90% of maximum heart rate or 8–9 on the i-Rate Scale, followed by running 3 minutes at an easy pace to recover. It is key to be disciplined and run the easy segments easy. Otherwise, the quality of your running and progressing is compromised. After the 1-minute repeats, run 5 minutes easy, then cool down.

*Pickups:* Run the workout at an easy pace and include three or four short, 30-second pickups within the run. Pick up your pace to a challenging pace where you can hear your breathing and it feels just outside your comfort zone. This is NOT at all-out gut-wrenching pace, simply one more notch up from where you were running. Keep the pickup to 30 seconds maximum. Your effort level should be 8 on the i-Rate Scale or 80% of maximum heart rate.

*Cross-training:* Include activities that are nonrunning or walking. Cycling, swimming, Pilates/yoga, strength training, elliptical training, stairclimbing, and Spinning are great cross-training modes for 5-K training. Cross-training allows you to rest your running muscles while training opposing muscle groups and reducing the risk of overtraining and injury. It helps speed recovery and reduces burnout. (See strength-training exercises in Chapter 14.) Cross-training activities should be done at a moderate pace at an i-Rate level of 6–7 or 60–70% of maximum heart rate.

## RUNNING FOR MORTALS 10-K WALK-RUN TRAINING PROGRAM

The 10-K Walk-Run Training Program is best suited for those who have been walk-running 40 minutes three or four times per week for at least 4 months or runners who have just completed the 5-K Walk-Run Training Program or a race and want to progress to a longer distance.

| Day | Monday | Tuesday | Wednesday |
|---|---|---|---|
| MODE | Walk-run | Cross-train or Rest | Walk-run |
| PACE OR INTENSITY | Conversational | Moderate | Conversational |
| I-RATE SCALE | 6.5–7.5 | 6–7 | 6.5–7.5 |
| HEART RATE | 65–75% | 60–70% | 65–75% |
| WEEK 1 | Run 2 min; walk 2 min. Repeat 10 times for a total of 40 min. | 30–45 min | Run 2 min; walk 2 min. Repeat 10 times for a total of 40 min. |
| WEEK 2 | Run 2 min; walk 2 min. Repeat 10 times for a total of 40 min. | 30–45 min | Run 2 min; walk 2 min. Repeat 10 times for a total of 40 min. |
| WEEK 3 | Run 2 min; walk 2 min. Repeat 10 times for a total of 40 min. | 30–45 min | Run 3 min; walk 2 min. Repeat 8 times for a total of 40 min. |
| WEEK 4 | Run 3 min; walk 2 min. Repeat 8 times for a total of 40 min. | 30–45 min | Run 3 min; walk 2 min. Repeat 8 times for a total of 40 min. |
| WEEK 5 | Run 3 min; walk 2 min. Repeat 8 times for a total of 40 min. | 30–45 min | Run 4 min; walk 2 min. Repeat 7 times for a total of 42 min. |
| WEEK 6 | Run 4 min; walk 2 min. Repeat 7 times for a total of 42 min. | 30–45 min | Run 4 min; walk 2 min. Repeat 7 times for a total of 42 min. |

| | Thursday | Friday | Saturday | Sunday |
|---|---|---|---|---|
| | Cross-train or Rest | Walk-run or Rest | Walk-run | Rest Day |
| | Moderate | Conversational | Conversational | |
| | 6–7 | 6.5–7.5 | 6.5–7.5 | |
| | 60–70% | 65–75% | 65–75% | |
| | 30–45 min | Rest | 40 min | Rest |
| | 30–45 min | Rest | Run 2 min; walk 2 min. Repeat 10 times for a total of 40 min. | Rest |
| | 30–45 min | Rest | Run 2 min; walk 2 min. Repeat 11 times for a total of 44 min. | Rest |
| | 30–45 min | Run 2 min; walk 2 min. Repeat 9 times for a total of 36 min. | Run 3 min; walk 2 min. Repeat 9 times for a total of 45 min. | Rest |
| | 30–45 min | Run 2 min; walk 2 min. Repeat 9 times for a total of 36 min. | Run 3 min; walk 2 min. Repeat 10 times for a total of 50 min. | Rest |
| | 30–45 min | Run 2 min; walk 2 min. Repeat 9 times for a total of 36 min. | Run 4 min; walk 2 min. Repeat 8 times for a total of 48 min. | Rest |

*(continued)*

## RUNNING FOR MORTALS 10-K WALK-RUN TRAINING PROGRAM (cont.)

| Day | Monday | Tuesday | Wednesday |
|---|---|---|---|
| MODE | Walk-run | Cross-train or Rest | Walk-run |
| PACE OR INTENSITY | Conversational | Moderate | Conversational |
| WEEK 7 | Run 4 min; walk 2 min. Repeat 7 times for a total of 42 min. | 30–45 min | Run 5 min; walk 2 min. Repeat 6 times for a total of 42 min. |
| WEEK 8 | Run 5 min; walk 2 min. Repeat 6 times for a total of 42 min. | 30–45 min | Run 5 min; walk 2 min. Repeat 7 times for a total of 49 min. |
| WEEK 9 | Run 5 min; walk 2 min. Repeat 6 times for a total of 42 min. | 30–45 min | Run 5 min; walk 1 min. Repeat 8 times for a total of 48 min. |
| WEEK 10 | Run 5 min; walk 1 min. Repeat 7 times for a total of 42 min. | Rest | Run 5 min; walk 1 min. Repeat 6 times for a total of 36 min. |
| POSTRACE WEEK | Run 5 min; walk 1 min. Repeat 6 times for a total of 36 min. | Rest | Run 5 min; walk 1 min. Repeat 7 times for a total of 42 min. |

Postrace is a perfect time to set another goal. If you want to maintain this program, continue repeating weeks 4–8. If you want to run more, follow the Run-Walk 10-K Training Program. If you want to run farther, follow the run-walk program in *Marathoning for Mortals* (Rodale, 2003).

### SCHEDULE KEY
**Walk-run workout**: Warm up by walking 5 minutes at a brisk pace. Run at a conversational pace (you can still talk) for prescribed number of minutes and follow with walking at a brisk pace for prescribed minutes. Example: Run 2 minutes; walk 2 minutes. Repeat sequence 10 times for a total of 40 minutes.

| Thursday | Friday | Saturday | Sunday |
|---|---|---|---|
| Cross-train or Rest | Walk-run or Rest | Walk-run | Rest Day |
| Moderate | Conversational | Conversational | |
| 30–45 min | Run 3 min; walk 2 min. Repeat 7 times for a total of 35 min. | Run 4 min; walk 2 min. Repeat 9 times for a total of 54 min. | Rest |
| 30–45 min | Run 3 min; walk 2 min. Repeat 7 times for a total of 35 min. | Run 5 min; walk 2 min. Repeat 8 times for a total of 56 min. | Rest |
| 30–45 min | Run 3 min; walk 2 min. Repeat 7 times for a total of 35 min. | Run 5 min; walk 1 min. Repeat 9 times for a total of 54 min. | Rest |
| 30 min | Rest | 10-K Race Run 5 min; walk 1 min start to finish | Rest |
| 30 min | Rest | 48 min | Rest |

*Cross-training:* Include activities that are nonrunning or walking. Cycling, swimming, Pilates/yoga, strength training, elliptical training, stairclimbing, and Spinning are great cross-training modes for 10-K training. Cross-training allows you to rest your running muscles while training opposing muscle groups and reducing the risk of overtraining and injury. It helps speed recovery and reduces burnout. (See strength-training exercises in Chapter 14.) Cross-training activities should be done at a moderate pace at an i-Rate level of 6–7 or 60–70% of maximum heart rate.

## RUNNING FOR MORTALS 10-K RUN-WALK TRAINING PROGRAM

The 10-K Run-Walk Training Program is best suited for those who have been run-walking three or four times per week, 40 to 45 minutes, for at least 4 months or those who have completed the 5-K Run-Walk Training Program or race and want to progress to a longer distance.

| Day | Monday | Tuesday | Wednesday |
|---|---|---|---|
| MODE | Run-walk | Cross-train or Rest | Run-walk |
| INTENSITY | Conversational Pace | Moderate | Conversational Pace |
| I-RATE SCALE | 6.5–7.5 | 6–7 | 6.5–7.5 |
| HEART RATE | 65–75% | 60–70% | 65–75% |
| WEEK 1 | Run 5 min; walk 1 min. Repeat 7 times for a total of 42 min. | 30–45 min | Run 5 min; walk 1 min. Repeat 7 times for a total of 42 min. |
| WEEK 2 | Run 5 min; walk 1 min. Repeat 7 times for a total of 42 min. | 30–45 min | Run 5 min; walk 1 min. Repeat 7 times for a total of 42 min. |
| WEEK 3 | Run 5 min; walk 1 min. Repeat 7 times for a total of 42 min. | 30–45 min | Run 5 min; walk 1 min. Repeat 8 times for a total of 48 min. |
| WEEK 4 | Run 6 min; walk 1 min. Repeat 6 times for a total of 42 min. | 30–45 min | Run 6 min; walk 1 min. Repeat 7 times for a total of 49 min. |
| WEEK 5 | Run 6 min; walk 1 min. Repeat 6 times for a total of 42 min. | 30–45 min | Run 6 min; walk 1 min. Repeat 7 times for a total of 49 min. |
| WEEK 6 | 49 min Run 6 min; walk 1 min. Repeat 7 times | 30–45 min | 48 min Run 7 min; walk 1 min. Repeat 6 times |

| Thursday | Friday | Saturday | Sunday |
|---|---|---|---|
| Cross-train or Rest | Run-walk or Rest | Run-walk | Rest Day |
| Moderate | Conversational Pace | Conversational Pace | |
| 6–7 | 6.5–7.5 | 6.5–7.5 | |
| 60–70% | 65–75% | 65–75% | |
| 30–45 min | Rest | Run 5 min; walk 1 min. Repeat 7 times for a total of 42 min. | Rest |
| 30–45 min | Rest | Run 5 min; walk 1 min. Repeat 7 times for a total of 42 min. | Rest |
| 30–45 min | Rest | Run 5 min; walk 1 min. Repeat 8 times for a total of 48 min. | Rest |
| 30–45 min | Run 5 min; walk 1 min. Repeat 6 times for a total of 36 min. | Run 6 min; walk 1 min. Repeat 7 times for a total of 49 min. | Rest |
| 30–45 min | Run 5 min; walk 1 min. Repeat 6 times for a total of 36 min. | Run 6 min; walk 1 min. Repeat 8 times for a total of 56 min. | Rest |
| 30–45 min | 36 min Run 5 min; walk 1 min. Repeat 6 times | 56 min Run 6 min; walk 1 min. Repeat 8 times | Rest |

*(continued)*

## RUNNING FOR MORTALS 10-K RUN-WALK TRAINING PROGRAM *(cont.)*

| Day | Monday | Tuesday | Wednesday |
|---|---|---|---|
| MODE | Run-walk | Cross-train or Rest | Run-walk |
| INTENSITY | Conversational Pace | Moderate | Conversational Pace |
| WEEK 7 | Run 7 min; walk 1 min. Repeat 6 times for a total of 48 min. | 30–45 min | Run 7 min; walk 1 min. Repeat 6 times for a total of 48 min. |
| WEEK 8 | Run 7 min; walk 1 min. Repeat 6 times for a total of 48 min. | 30–45 min | Run 8 min; walk 1 min. Repeat 5 times for a total of 45 min. |
| WEEK 9 | Run 8 min; walk 1 min. Repeat 5 times for a total of 45 min. | 30–45 min | Run 8 min; walk 1 min. Repeat 5 times for a total of 45 min. |
| WEEK 10 | Run 8 min; walk 1 min. Repeat 5 times for a total of 45 min. | Rest | Run 8 min; walk 1 min. Repeat 4 times for a total of 36 min. |
| POSTRACE WEEK | Run 8 min; walk 1 min. Repeat 4 times for a total of 36 min. | Rest | Run 8 min; walk 1 min. Repeat 5 times for a total of 45 min. |

Postrace is a perfect time to set another goal. If you want to maintain this program, continue repeating weeks 4–8. If you want to run more, follow the 10-K Run Training Program. If you want to run farther, follow the run-walk program in *Marathoning for Mortals* (Rodale, 2003).

**SCHEDULE KEY**
***Run-walk workout***: After the warmup, walk 5 minutes at a brisk pace. Run at a conversational pace (you can still talk) for prescribed number of minutes and follow with walking at a brisk pace for prescribed minutes. Example: Run 5 minutes; walk 1 minute. Repeat sequence five times for a total of 30 minutes.

| Thursday | Friday | Saturday | Sunday |
|---|---|---|---|
| Cross-train or Rest | Run-walk or Rest | Run-walk | Rest Day |
| Moderate | Conversational Pace | Conversational Pace | |
| 30–45 min | Run 5 min; walk 1 min. Repeat 6 times for a total of 36 min. | Run 7 min; walk 1 min. Repeat 7 times for a total of 56 min. | Rest |
| 30–45 min | Run 5 min; walk 1 min. Repeat 6 times for a total of 36 min. | Run 7 min; walk 1 min. Repeat 8 times for a total of 64 min. | Rest |
| 30–45 min | Run 5 min; walk 1 min. Repeat 6 times for a total of 36 min. | Run 8 min; walk 1 min. Repeat 6 times for a total of 54 min. | Rest |
| 30 min | Rest | 10-K Race Walk 1 minute at every mile start to finish | Rest |
| 30 min | Rest | Run 8 min; walk 1 min. Repeat 5 times for a total of 45 min. | Rest |

*Cross-training:* Include activities that are nonrunning or walking. Cycling, swimming, Pilates/yoga, strength training, elliptical training, stairclimbing, and Spinning are great cross-training modes for 10-K training. Cross-training allows you to rest your running muscles while training opposing muscle groups and reducing the risk of overtraining and injury. It helps speed recovery and reduces burnout. (See strength-training exercises in Chapter 14.) Cross-training activities should be done at a moderate pace at an i-Rate level of 6–7 or 60–70% of maximum heart rate.

## RUNNING FOR MORTALS 10-K RUN TRAINING PROGRAM

The 10-K Run Training Program is best suited for those who have been running 40–50 minutes at least three or four times per week for at least 6 months.

| Day | Monday | Tuesday | Wednesday |
|---|---|---|---|
| MODE | Run | Cross-train or Rest | Run + *Pickups |
| PACE OR INTENSITY | Conversational | Moderate | Moderate + Challenging |
| I-RATE SCALE | 6.5–7.5 | 6–7 | 8 |
| HEART RATE | 65–75% | 60–70% | 80% |
| WEEK 1 | 40 min | 30–40 min | 40 min |
| WEEK 2 | 40 min | 30–40 min | 40 min |
| WEEK 3 | 40 min | 30–40 min | 40 min |
| WEEK 4 | 40 min | 30–40 min | 45 min |
| WEEK 5 | 45 min | 30–40 min | 45 min |
| WEEK 6 | 45 min | 30–40 min | 45 min |
| WEEK 7 | 45 min | 30–40 min | 50 min |
| WEEK 8 | 45 min | 30–40 min | 50 min |
| WEEK 9 | 45 min | 30–40 min | 45 min |
| WEEK 10 | 40 min | Rest | 30 min |
| POSTRACE WEEK | 35 min | Rest | 40 min |

Postrace is a perfect time to set another goal. If you want to maintain this program, continue repeating weeks 4–8. If you want to improve time, follow the Advanced Run Training Program. If you want to run farther, follow *Marathoning for Mortals* (Rodale, 2003).

### SCHEDULE KEY

**Run workout:** After the warmup, walk 5 minutes at a brisk pace. Run at a conversational pace (you can still talk) at an i-Rate level of 6–7 or, if you are using a heart rate monitor, at 65–75% of maximum heart rate.

**\*Pickups:** Run the workout at an easy pace and include four to six short, 30-second pickups within the run. Pick up your pace to a challenging pace where you can hear your breathing and it feels just outside your comfort zone. This is NOT at all-out gut-wrenching pace, simply one more notch up from where you were running. Keep the pickup to 30 seconds maximum. Your effort level should be 8 on the i-Rate Scale or 80% of maximum heart rate.

| Thursday | Friday | Saturday | Sunday |
|---|---|---|---|
| Cross-train or Rest | Run | Run | Rest Day |
| Moderate | Conversational | Conversational | |
| 6–7 | 6.5–7.5 | 6.5–7.5 | |
| 60–70% | 65–75% | 65–75% | |
| 30–40 min | Rest | 45 min | Rest |
| 30–40 min | Rest | 45 min | Rest |
| 30–40 min | Rest | 50 min | Rest |
| 30–40 min | 30 min | 55 min | Rest |
| 30–40 min | 30 min | 45 min | Rest |
| 30–40 min | 30 min | 60 min | Rest |
| 30–40 min | 40 min | 50 min | Rest |
| 30–40 min | 40 min | 70 min | Rest |
| 30–40 min | 30 min | 45 min | Rest |
| Rest | Rest | 10-K Race | Rest |
| 30 min | Rest | 45 min | Rest |

*Cross-training:* Include activities that are nonrunning or walking. Cycling, swimming, Pilates/yoga, strength training, elliptical training, stairclimbing, and Spinning are great cross-training modes for 10-K training. Cross-training allows you to rest your running muscles while training opposing muscle groups and reducing the risk of overtraining and injury. It helps speed recovery and reduces burnout. (See strength-training exercises in Chapter 14.) Cross-training activities should be done at a moderate pace at an i-Rate level of 6–7 or 60–70% of maximum heart rate.

*Flexibility:* Stretch after every workout when the muscles are warm to maintain or improve flexibility and prevent injuries. (See flexibility stretches in Chapter 13.)

## RUNNING FOR MORTALS 10-K ADVANCED RUN TRAINING PROGRAM

The 10-K Advanced Run Training Program is best suited for those who have been running 45–60 minutes at least four or five times per week for at least 1 year.

| Day | Monday | Tuesday | Wednesday |
|---|---|---|---|
| MODE | Run | Cross-train or Rest | Run |
| PACE OR INTENSITY | Conversational | Moderate | Challenging |
| I-RATE SCALE | 6.5–7.5 | 6–7 | 8–9 |
| HEART RATE | 65–75% | 60–70% | 80–90% |
| WEEK 1 | 40 min | 30–45 min | 50 min *Pickups |
| WEEK 2 | 40 min | 30–45 min | 50 min *Pickups |
| WEEK 3 | 40 min | 30–45 min | 55 min *Pickups |
| WEEK 4 | 45 min | 30–45 min | 55 min *Speed A workout |
| WEEK 5 | 45 min | 30–45 min | 45 min *Speed A workout |
| WEEK 6 | 45 min | 30–45 min | 55 min *Speed B workout |
| WEEK 7 | 45 min | 30–45 min | 55 min *Speed B workout |
| WEEK 8 | 45 min | 30–45 min | 55 min *Speed C workout |
| WEEK 9 | 45 min | 30–45 min | 55 min *Speed C workout |
| WEEK 10 | 40 min | Rest | 40 min *Speed D workout |
| POSTRACE WEEK | 40 min | Rest | 40 min |

Postrace is a perfect time to set another goal. If you want to maintain this program, continue repeating weeks 4–8. If you want to run longer races, follow the run programs in *Marathoning for Mortals* (Rodale, 2003).

| Thursday | Friday | Saturday | Sunday |
|---|---|---|---|
| Cross-train or Rest | Run | Run | Rest Day |
| Moderate | Conversational | Conversational | |
| 6–7 | 6.5–7.5 | 6.5–7.5 | |
| 60–70% | 65–75% | 65–75% | |
| 30–45 min | 40 min | 45 min | Rest |
| 30–45 min | 40 min | 45 min | Rest |
| 30–45 min | 40 min | 50 min | Rest |
| 30–45 min | 40 min | 50 min | Rest |
| 30–45 min | 40 min | 45 min | Rest |
| 30–45 min | 40 min | 60 min | Rest |
| 30–45 min | 40 min | 50 min | Rest |
| 30–45 min | 40 min | 70 min | Rest |
| 30–45 min | 40 min | 45 min | Rest |
| Rest | 30 min | 10-K Race | Rest |
| 30–40 min | Rest | 45 min | Rest |

(continued)

# RUNNING FOR MORTALS 10-K ADVANCED RUN TRAINING PROGRAM *(cont.)*

**SCHEDULE KEY**

*Advanced run workout*: After the warmup, walk 5 minutes at a brisk pace. Run at a conversational pace (you can still talk) at an i-Rate level of 6–7 or, if you are using a heart rate monitor, at 65–75% of maximum heart rate.

*\*Speed A workout:* After the warmup, walk 5 minutes at a brisk pace. Run 10 minutes at an easy pace. Then repeat the following five times: Run 2 minutes hard at 85–90% of maximum heart rate or 8–9 on the i-Rate Scale, followed by running 4 minutes at an easy pace to recover. It is key to be disciplined and run the easy segments easy. Otherwise, the quality of your running and progressing is compromised. After the 2-minute repeats, run 5 minutes easy, then cool down.

*\*Speed B workout:* After the warmup, walk 5 minutes at a brisk pace. Run 10 minutes at an easy pace. Then repeat the following five times: Run 3 minutes hard at 85–90% of maximum heart rate or 8–9 on the i-Rate Scale, followed by running 3 minutes at an easy pace to recover. It is key to be disciplined and run the easy segments easy. Otherwise, the quality of your running and progressing is compromised. After the 3-minute repeats, run 5 minutes easy, then cool down.

*\*Speed C workout:* After the warmup, walk 5 minutes at a brisk pace. Run 5 minutes at an easy pace. Then repeat the following three times: Run 10 minutes at a comfortably hard pace at 80–85% of maximum heart rate or 8–8.5 on the i-Rate Scale, followed by running 2 minutes at an easy pace to recover. It is key to be disciplined and run the easy segments easy. Otherwise, the quality of your running and progressing is compromised. After the 10-minute repeats, run 5 minutes easy, then cool down.

*Speed D workout:* After the warmup, walk 5 minutes at a brisk pace. Run 10 minutes at an easy pace. Then repeat the following four times: Run 1 minute hard at 85–90% of maximum heart rate or 8–9 on the i-Rate Scale, followed by running 3 minutes at an easy pace to recover. It is key to be disciplined and run the easy segments easy. Otherwise, the quality of your running and progressing is compromised. After the 1-minute repeats, run 5 minutes easy, then cool down.

*Pickups:* Run the workout at an easy pace and include six to eight short, 30-second pickups within the run. Pick up your pace to a challenging pace where you can hear your breathing and it feels just outside your comfort zone. This is NOT at all-out gut-wrenching pace, simply one more notch up from where you were running. Keep the pickup to 30 seconds maximum. Your effort level should be 8 on the i-Rate Scale or 80% of maximum heart rate.

*Cross-training:* Include activities that are nonrunning or walking. Cycling, swimming, Pilates/yoga, strength training, elliptical training, stairclimbing, and Spinning are great cross-training modes for 5-K training. Cross-training allows you to rest your running muscles while training opposing muscle groups and reducing the risk of overtraining and injury. It helps speed recovery and reduces burnout. (See strength-training exercises in Chapter 14.) Cross-training activities should be done at a moderate pace at an i-Rate level of 6–7 or 60–70% of maximum heart rate.

## RUNNING FOR MORTALS WEIGHT LOSS PROGRAM:
### PHASE I

Phase I is geared toward those who have been inactive for the past 3 months or more. For the best results, start here if you have not exercised regularly in the past 3 months or more, then progress through to Phases II and III.

| Day | Monday | Tuesday | Wednesday |
|---|---|---|---|
| MODE | Walk/Walk-run | Strength Train | Walk *Pickups |
| PACE OR INTENSITY | Conversational | 1 Set, 15 Reps | Conversational + Challenging |
| I-RATE SCALE | 6.5–7.5 | | 7–8 |
| HEART RATE | 65–75% | | 70–80% |
| WEEK 1 | Walk 30 min | 30–40 min | 30 min |
| WEEK 2 | Walk 35 min | 30–40 min | 30 min |
| WEEK 3 | Walk 40 min | 30–40 min | 30 min |
| WEEK 4 | Walk 3 min; run 1 min. Repeat 8 times for a total of 32 min. | 30–40 min | 35 min *Pickups |
| WEEK 5 | Walk 3 min; run 1 min. Repeat 8 times for a total of 32 min. | 30–40 min | 35 min *Pickups |
| WEEK 6 | Walk 4 min; run 1 min. Repeat 7 times for a total of 35 min. | 30–40 min | 35 min *Pickups |
| WEEK 7 | Walk 4 min; run 1 min. Repeat 7 times for a total of 35 min. | 30–40 min | 40 min *Pickups |
| WEEK 8 | Walk 3 min; run 1 min. Repeat 10 times for a total of 40 min. | 30–40 min | 40 min *Pickups |

| | Thursday | Friday | Saturday | Sunday |
|---|---|---|---|---|
| | Strength Train | Walk/Walk-run | Walk | Rest Day |
| | 1 Set, 15 Reps | Conversational | Conversational | |
| | | 6.5–7.5 | 6–7 | |
| | | 65–75% | 60–70% | |
| | 30–40 min | Walk 30 min | 30 min | Rest |
| | 30–40 min | Walk 30 min | 30 min | Rest |
| | 30–40 min | Walk 30 min | 35 min | Rest |
| | 30–40 min | Walk 30 min | 35 min | Rest |
| | 30–40 min | Walk 3 min; run 1 min. Repeat 8 times for a total of 32 min. | 40 min | Rest |
| | 30–40 min | Walk 3 min; run 1 min. Repeat 8 times for a total of 32 min. | 40 min | Rest |
| | 30–40 min | Walk 4 min; run 1 min. Repeat 6 times for a total of 30 min. | 50 min | Rest |
| | 30–40 min | Walk 4 min; run 1 min. Repeat 6 times for a total of 30 min. | 50 min | Rest |

*(continued)*

## RUNNING FOR MORTALS WEIGHT LOSS PROGRAM:
## PHASE I *(cont.)*

| Day | Monday | Tuesday | Wednesday |
|---|---|---|---|
| MODE | Walk/Walk-run | Strength Train | Walk *Pickups |
| PACE OR INTENSITY | Conversational | 1 Set, 15 Reps | Conversational + Challenging |
| WEEK 9 | Walk 3 min; run 2 min. Repeat 11 times for a total of 44 min. | 30–40 min | 45 min *Pickups |
| WEEK 10 | Walk 3 min; run 2 min. Repeat 8 times for a total of 40 min. | 30–40 min | Walk 2 min; run 2 min. Repeat 9 times for a total of 36 min. |
| WEEK 11 | Walk 3 min; run 2 min. Repeat 8 times for a total of 40 min. | 30–40 min | Walk 2 min; run 3 min. Repeat 7 times for a total of 35 min. |
| WEEK 12 | Walk 2 min; run 3 min. Repeat 9 times for a total of 45 min. | 30–40 min | Walk 2 min; run 3 min. Repeat 7 times for a total of 35 min. |

**Walk workout:** Walk at a conversational pace (you can still talk) at an i-Rate level of 6–7 or, if you are using a heart rate monitor, at 60–70% of maximum heart rate. This pace should be one notch above your easy warmup pace or a level at which you are breathing a little more vigorously.

**Walk-run workout:** After the warmup, walk 5 minutes at a brisk pace. Run at a conversational pace (you can still talk) for prescribed number of minutes and follow with walking at a brisk pace for prescribed minutes. Example: Walk 3 minutes; run 1 minute. Repeat sequence eight times for a total of 32 minutes.

**\*Pickups:** Walk the workout at an easy pace and include three or four short, 30-second pickups within the workout. Pick up your pace to a challenging pace where you can hear your breathing and it feels just outside your comfort zone. This is NOT at all-out gut-wrenching pace, simply one more notch up from where you were walking. Keep the pickup to 30 seconds maximum. Your effort level should be at an i-Rate Scale of 8 or 80% of maximum heart rate.

| Thursday | Friday | Saturday | Sunday |
|---|---|---|---|
| Strength Train | Walk/Walk-run | Walk | Rest Day |
| 1 Set, 15 Reps | Conversational | Conversational | |
| 30–40 min | Walk 2 min; run 2 min. Repeat 7 times for a total of 28 min. | 60 min | Rest |
| 30–40 min | Walk 2 min; run 2 min. Repeat 7 times for a total of 28 min. | 60 min | Rest |
| 30–40 min | Walk 2 min; run 3 min. Repeat 6 times for a total of 30 min. | 60 min | Rest |
| 30–40 min | Walk 2 min; run 3 min. Repeat 6 times for a total of 30 min. | 60 min | Rest |

*Strength training:* Strength train with machines, weights, or resistance tubes/bands or classes like Pilates, toning, or yoga. Consider working with a personal trainer. There are many ways to include resistance training in your life; find the one you enjoy the most. Include strength-training exercises for your upper body, core (abdominal and trunk), and lower body twice per week. This will increase the lean muscle tissue, boost metabolism at rest, and prevent the dreaded muscle loss with age. The more muscle we lose, the lower our metabolism sinks. Start the strength-training session by warming up with 10 minutes of cardio activity (e.g., cycling, elliptical training, or stairclimbing). Perform the strength-training exercises in Phase III: One set per exercise, 15 repetitions per set. Your goal is to fatigue the muscle as you reach the 15th rep or can no longer perform the exercise with good, controlled form. Select the proper weight or resistance to accomplish this effectively.

## RUNNING FOR MORTALS WEIGHT LOSS PROGRAM:
### PHASE II

Phase II is geared toward those who have completed Phase I or have been exercising three or four times per week for at least 3 months.

| DAY | Monday | Tuesday | Wednesday |
|---|---|---|---|
| MODE | Run-walk | Strength Train | Run-walk |
| PACE OR INTENSITY | Conversational | 2–3 Sets, 15 Reps | Conversational |
| I-RATE SCALE | 6.5–7.5 | | 6.5–7.5 |
| HEART RATE | 65–75% | | 65–75% |
| WEEK 1 | Run 3 min; walk 2 min. Repeat 8 times for a total of 40 min. | 40 min | Run 3 min; walk 2 min. Repeat 8 times for a total of 40 min. |
| WEEK 2 | Run 3 min; walk 2 min. Repeat 8 times for a total of 40 min. | 40 min | Run 3 min; walk 2 min. Repeat 8 times for a total of 40 min. |
| WEEK 3 | Run 3 min; walk 2 min. Repeat 8 times for a total of 40 min. | 40 min | Run 3 min; walk 2 min. Repeat 8 times for a total of 40 min. |
| WEEK 4 | Run 3 min; walk 2 min. Repeat 8 times for a total of 40 min. | 40 min | Run 4 min; walk 2 min. Repeat 7 times for a total of 42 min. |
| WEEK 5 | Run 4 min; walk 2 min. Repeat 7 times for a total of 42 min. | 40 min | Run 4 min; walk 2 min. Repeat 7 times for a total of 42 min. |
| WEEK 6 | Run 4 min; walk 2 min. Repeat 7 times for a total of 42 min. | 40 min | Run 5 min; walk 2 min. Repeat 6 times for a total of 42 min. |
| WEEK 7 | Run 5 min; walk 2 min. Repeat 6 times for a total of 42 min. | 40 min | Run 5 min; walk 2 min. Repeat 6 times for a total of 42 min. |

| Thursday | Friday | Saturday | Sunday |
|---|---|---|---|
| Strength Train | Walk | Run-walk | Rest Day |
| 2–3 Sets, 15 Reps | Conversational | Conversational | |
| | 6.5–7.5 | 6–7 | |
| | 65–75% | 60–70% | |
| 40 min | 60 min | Run 3 min; walk 2 min. Repeat 9 times for a total of 45 min. | Rest |
| 40 min | 60 min | Run 3 min; walk 2 min. Repeat 9 times for a total of 45 min. | Rest |
| 40 min | 60 min | Run 4 min; walk 2 min. Repeat 8 times for a total of 48 min. | Rest |
| 40 min | 60 min | Run 4 min; walk 2 min. Repeat 8 times for a total of 48 min. | Rest |
| 40 min | 60 min | Run 5 min; walk 2 min. Repeat 7 times for a total of 49 min. | Rest |
| 40 min | 60 min | Run 5 min; walk 2 min. Repeat 7 times for a total of 49 min. | Rest |
| 40 min | 60 min | Run 6 min; walk 2 min. Repeat 6 times for a total of 48 min. | Rest |

*(continued)*

## RUNNING FOR MORTALS WEIGHT LOSS PROGRAM:
### PHASE II *(cont.)*

| DAY | Monday | Tuesday | Wednesday |
|---|---|---|---|
| MODE | Run-walk | Strength Train | Run-walk |
| PACE OR INTENSITY | Conversational | 2–3 Sets, 15 Reps | Conversational |
| WEEK 8 | Run 5 min; walk 2 min. Repeat 6 times for a total of 42 min. | 40 min | Run 6 min; walk 2 min. Repeat 6 times for a total of 48 min. |
| WEEK 9 | Run 6 min; walk 2 min. Repeat 6 times for a total of 48 min. | 40 min | Run 6 min; walk 2 min. Repeat 6 times for a total of 48 min. |
| WEEK 10 | Run 6 min; walk 2 min. Repeat 5 times for a total of 40 min. | 40 min | Run 6 min; walk 1 min. Repeat 7 times for a total of 49 min. |
| WEEK 11 | Run 6 min; walk 1 min. Repeat 6 times for a total of 42 min. | 40 min | Run 6 min; walk 1 min. Repeat 7 times for a total of 49 min. |
| WEEK 12 | Run 6 min; walk 1 min. Repeat 6 times for a total of 42 min. | 40 min | Run 7 min; walk 1 min. Repeat 6 times for a total of 48 min. |

**Workout:** After the warmup, walk 5 minutes at a brisk pace. Run at a conversational pace (you can still talk) for prescribed number of minutes and follow with walking at a brisk pace for prescribed minutes. Example: Run-walk: Run 3 minutes; walk 2 minutes. Repeat sequence eight times for a total of 40 minutes.

**Strength training**: Strength train with machines, weights, or resistance tubes/bands or classes like Pilates, toning, or yoga. Consider working with a personal trainer. There are many ways to include resistance training in your life; find the one

| Thursday | Friday | Saturday | Sunday |
|---|---|---|---|
| Strength Train | Walk | Run-walk | Rest Day |
| 2–3 Sets, 15 Reps | Conversational | Conversational | |
| 40 min | 60 min | Run 6 min; walk 2 min. Repeat 6 times for a total of 48 min. | Rest |
| 40 min | 60 min | Run 6 min; walk 1 min. Repeat 7 times for a total of 49 min. | Rest |
| 40 min | 60 min | Run 6 min; walk 1 min. Repeat 7 times for a total of 49 min. | Rest |
| 40 min | 60 min | Run 7 min; walk 1 min. Repeat 6 times for a total of 48 min. | Rest |
| 40 min | 60 min | Run 7 min; walk 1 min. Repeat 6 times for a total of 48 min. | Rest |

you enjoy the most. This will increase the lean muscle tissue, boost metabolism at rest, and prevent the dreaded muscle loss with age. Start the strength-training session by warming up with 10 minutes of cardio activity (e.g., cycling, elliptical training, or stairclimbing). Perform strength-training exercises in Phase III: two or three sets per exercise, 15 repetitions per set. Your goal is to fatigue the muscle as you reach the 15th rep or can no longer perform the exercise with good, controlled form. Select the proper weight or resistance to effectively accomplish this.

## RUNNING FOR MORTALS WEIGHT LOSS PROGRAM:
### PHASE III

Phase III is geared toward those who have completed Phase II or have been running regularly three or four times per week for at least 3 months. This phase incorporates circuit training, metabolism boosters, and continuous running to enhance weight loss or maintain a healthy weight.

| Day | Monday | Tuesday | Wednesday |
|---|---|---|---|
| MODE | Run | Strength Circuit Workout | Run/*Pickups |
| PACE OR INTENSITY | Conversational | 1 Set, 8–12 Reps | Conversational + Challenging |
| I-RATE SCALE | 6.5–7.5 | | 7–8.5 |
| HEART RATE | 65–75% | | 70–85% |
| WEEK 1 | 30 min | 45 min Circuit workout | Run 8 min; walk 1 min. Repeat 5 times for a total of 45 min. |
| WEEK 2 | 30 min | 45 min Circuit workout | Run 8 min; walk 1 min. Repeat 5 times for a total of 45 min. |
| WEEK 3 | 30 min | 45 min Circuit workout | Run 8 min; walk 1 min. Repeat 5 times for a total of 45 min. |
| WEEK 4 | 35 min | 45 min Circuit workout | Run 9 min; walk 1 min. Repeat 5 times for a total of 50 min. |
| WEEK 5 | 35 min | 45 min Circuit workout | Run 9 min; walk 1 min. Repeat 5 times for a total of 50 min. |
| WEEK 6 | 35 min | 45 min Circuit workout | 45 min 50 min. Repeat 5 times |
| WEEK 7 | 40 min | 45 min Circuit workout | 45 min *Pickups |

| | Thursday | Friday | Saturday | Sunday |
|---|---|---|---|---|
| | Strength Train | Double Burn: Run + Walk | Run | Rest Day |
| | 2–3 Sets, 8–12 Reps | Conversational | Conversational | |
| | | 6.5–7.5 | 6.5–7.5 | |
| | | 65–75% | 65–75% | |
| | 40 min | a.m.: Run 30 min<br>p.m.: Walk 30 min | 35 min | Rest |
| | 40 min | a.m.: Run 30 min<br>p.m.: Walk 30 min | 35 min | Rest |
| | 40 min | a.m.: Run 30 min<br>p.m.: Walk 30 min | 40 min | Rest |
| | 40 min | a.m.: Run 30 min<br>p.m.: Walk 30 min | 40 min | Rest |
| | 40 min | a.m.: Run 30 min<br>p.m.: Walk 30 min | 40 min | Rest |
| | 40 min | a.m.: Run 30 min<br>p.m.: Walk 30 min | 45 min | Rest |
| | 40 min | a.m.: Run 30 min<br>p.m.: Walk 30 min | 45 min | Rest |

*(continued)*

# RUNNING FOR MORTALS WEIGHT LOSS PROGRAM: PHASE III (cont.)

| Day | Monday | Tuesday | Wednesday |
|---|---|---|---|
| MODE | Run | Strength Circuit Workout | Run/*Pickups |
| PACE OR INTENSITY | Conversational | 1 Set, 8–12 Reps | Conversational + Challenging |
| WEEK 8 | 40 min | 45 min Circuit workout | 45 min *Pickups |
| WEEK 9 | 40 min | 45 min Circuit workout | 45 min *Pickups |
| WEEK 10 | 40 min *Hilly run | 45 min Circuit workout | 45 min *Pickups |
| WEEK 11 | 40 min *Hilly run | 45 min Circuit workout | 50 min *Pickups |
| WEEK 12 | 45 min *Hilly run | 45 min Circuit workout | 50 min *Pickups |

**Run-walk workout:** After the warmup, walk 5 minutes at a brisk pace. Run at a conversational pace (you can still talk) for prescribed number of minutes and follow with walking at a brisk pace for prescribed minutes. Example: Run 8 minutes; walk 1 minute. Repeat sequence five times for a total of 45 minutes.

**\*Pickups**: Run the workout at an easy pace and include six to eight short, 30-second pickups within the run. Pick up your pace to a challenging pace where you can hear your breathing and it feels just outside your comfort zone. This is NOT at all-out gut-wrenching pace, simply one more notch up from where you were running. Keep the pickup to 30 seconds maximum. Your effort level should be 8 on the i-Rate Scale or 80% of maximum heart rate.

**Run workout:** After the warmup, walk 5 minutes at a brisk pace. Run at conversational pace (you can still talk) at an i-Rate level of 6–7 or, if you are using a heart rate monitor, at 65–75% of maximum heart rate.

**Hilly run:** After the warmup, walk 5 minutes at a brisk pace. Incorporate three or four rolling hills in your run. Whether outdoors or on the treadmill, adding hills increases heart rate and calories burned. It is also a great way to strengthen your legs. Start with three hills and add another hill each week.

**Double fun—run + walk:** Including a 30-minute walk at night will boost your metabolism twice that day and burn more calories. Walk the dog, take a family stroll after dinner, or even walk around the block a few times. It doesn't need to be hard; an easy walk will boost metabolism one last time.

**Strength training:** Strength train with machines, weights, or resistance tubes/bands or classes like Pilates, toning, or yoga. Consider working with a personal trainer. There are many ways to include resistance training in your life; find the one

| Thursday | Friday | Saturday | Sunday |
|---|---|---|---|
| Strength Train | Double Burn: Run + Walk | Run | Rest Day |
| 2–3 Sets, 8–12 Reps | Conversational | Conversational | |
| 40 min | a.m.: Run 30 min<br>p.m.: Walk 30 min | 45 min | Rest |
| 40 min | a.m.: Run 30 min<br>p.m.: Walk 30 min | 50 min | Rest |
| 40 min | a.m.: Run 30 min<br>p.m.: Walk 30 min | 50 min | Rest |
| 40 min | a.m.: Run 30 min<br>p.m.: Walk 30 min | 50 min | Rest |
| 40 min | a.m.: Run 30 min<br>p.m.: Walk 30 min | 60 min | Rest |

you enjoy the most. Include strength-training exercises for your upper body, core (abdominals and trunk), and lower body twice per week. Start the strength-training session by warming up with 10 minutes of cardio activity (e.g., cycling, elliptical training, or stairclimbing). Perform the strength-training exercises below: two or three sets per exercise, 8–12 repetitions per set. Your goal is to fatigue the muscle within 8–12 reps or until you can no longer perform the exercise with good, controlled form. Select the proper weight or resistance to effectively accomplish this.

*Strength circuit workout:* Warm up with 10 minutes of cycling, stairclimbing, or another cardio machine other than a treadmill. Perform two or three sets of 8–12 reps for each muscle group in your arms (biceps, triceps, shoulders), then do 5 more minutes of cardio activity at a moderate pace, or 60–70% of maximum heart rate or level 6–7 on the i-Rate Scale. Perform one set of 8–12 reps of two to four exercises for each muscle group in your chest and back (e.g., pushup, chest press, lat pull, row), then do 5 more minutes of cardio activity at a moderate pace. Perform one set of 8–12 reps of three or four exercises for each lower-body muscle group (e.g., lunge, squat, leg curl, hip extension), then do 5 minutes of cardio activity at a moderate pace. Perform one set of 15–20 reps of three or four core exercises for abdominals and low back (e.g., crunches, Superman, plank). It is key to move from one exercise to another as quickly as possible, making the workout more demanding and burning more calories. Finish the workout with flexibility exercises.

*Metabolism boosters:* Begin to incorporate metabolism microbursts into your everyday life. Use stairs instead of escalators or elevators; park farther away from entrances at work, school, or stores; walk to deliver memos instead of e-mailing them to coworkers. Get a pedometer and see how many steps you take (outside of running) during an average day. Shoot for 5,000–8,000 steps every day. These energy burners add up to help reduce or maintain your weight.

# INDEX

Boldface page references indicate photographs.
Underscored references indicate tables or boxed text.